WITHDRAWN
UTSA Libraries

The Discourse
of Classified Advertising

OXFORD STUDIES IN SOCIOLINGUISTICS
Edward Finegan, *General Editor*

Editorial Advisory Board
Douglas Biber
Alessandro Duranti
John R. Rickford
Suzanne Romaine
Deborah Tannen

Locating Dialect in Discourse
The Language of Honest Men and Bonnie Lassies in Ayr
RONALD K.S. MACAULAY

English in Its Social Contexts
Essays in Historical Sociolinguistics
EDITED BY TIM W. MACHAN AND CHARLES T. SCOTT

Coherence in Psychotic Discourse
BRANCA TELLES RIBEIRO

Sociolinguistic Perspectives on Register
EDITED BY DOUGLAS BIBER AND EDWARD FINEGAN

Gender and Conversational Interaction
EDITED BY DEBORAH TANNEN

Therapeutic Ways with Words
KATHLEEN WARDEN FERRARA

The Linguistic Individual
Self-Expression in Language and Linguistics
BARBARA JOHNSTONE

The Discourse of Classified Advertising
Exploring the Nature of Linguistic Simplicity
PAUL BRUTHIAUX

The Discourse of Classified Advertising

Exploring the Nature of Linguistic Simplicity

PAUL BRUTHIAUX

New York   Oxford
OXFORD UNIVERSITY PRESS
1996

Oxford University Press

Oxford   New York
Athens   Auckland   Bangkok
Calcutta   Cape Town   Dar es Salaam   Delhi
Florence   Hong Kong   Istanbul   Karachi
Kuala Lumpur   Madras   Madrid   Melbourne
Mexico City   Nairobi   Paris   Singapore
Taipei   Tokyo   Toronto

and associated companies in
Berlin   Ibadan

Copyright © 1996 by Paul Bruthiaux

Published by Oxford University Press, Inc.
198 Madison Avenue, New York, New York 10016

Oxford is a registered trademark of Oxford University Press, Inc.

All rights reserved. No part of this publication may be reproduced,
stored in a retrieval system, or transmitted, in any form or by any means,
electronic, mechanical, photocopying, recording or otherwise,
without the prior permission of Oxford University Press.

Library of Congress Cataloging-in-Publication Data
Bruthiaux, Paul.
  The discourse of classified advertising : exploring the nature of
linguistic simplicity / Paul Bruthiaux.
      p.   cm.—(Oxford studies in sociolinguistics)
  Includes bibliographical references and index.
  ISBN 0-19-510032-8
  1. Advertising—Language.   2. Advertising, Classified.   3. English
language—Usage.   I. Title.   II. Series.
HF5827.B75   1996
659.13'2—dc20   95-41493

9 8 7 6 5 4 3 2 1

Printed in the United States of America
on acid-free paper

SERIES FOREWORD

Simply put, sociolinguistics is the study of language in use. With special focus on the relationships between language and society, sociolinguistics addresses the forms and functions of variation across social groups and across the range of communicative situations in which speakers and writers deploy their verbal repertoires. In short, sociolinguistics examines discourse as it is constructed and co-constructed, shaped and reshaped, in the interactions of everyday life and as it creates and reflects the social realities of that life.

Some linguists examine the structure of sentences independent of who is speaking or writing and to whom, independent of what precedes and what follows in the discourse, and independent of setting, topic, and purpose, but sociolinguists and discourse analysts investigate linguistic expression in its social and situational contexts. Among observers who are *not* professional linguists, interest likewise focuses on language in discourse, for it is there that the patterns of social structure and strategic enterprise that engage the attention of so many people are mirrored.

Offering a platform for studies of language use in communities around the globe, Oxford Studies in Sociolinguistics invites synchronic or diachronic treatments of social dialects and registers, of oral, written, or signed discourse. The series welcomes studies that are descriptive or theoretical, interpretive or analytical. While its volumes usually report original research, an occasional one synthesizes or interprets existing knowledge. The series aims for a style that is accessible beyond linguists to other humanists and social scientists, and some volumes may appeal to educated readers keenly interested in the language of human affairs—for example, the discourse of doctors or lawyers engaging clients and one another with specialist registers or, as in the volume at hand, of women and men selling cars, renting apartments, and seeking friendship and love through classified advertisements. By providing a forum for innovative studies of language in use, Oxford Studies in Sociolinguistics aims to influence the agenda for linguistic research in the 21st century and provide an array of provocative analyses to help launch that agenda.

In *The Discourse of Classified Advertising*, Paul Bruthiaux provides a detailed analysis of linguistic forms and communicative functions in four types of ads: automobile sales, apartment rentals, job vacancies, and personals. Focusing on gauges of simplicity, he pointedly refers to certain characteristic features as "simple" rather than "simplified." Besides similarities among diverse "simple" registers, he notes differences in the kinds of simplicity characteristic of ad types and links them to communicative functions. Giving emphasis to conventionalized features in ads, Bruthiaux argues for a view of discourse in which prefabricated chunks play a more significant role than is typically assumed in current grammatical theories. Along with a detailed analysis of 800 classified ads, Bruthiaux offers arguments for modified views of simplicity and of the role of convention in discourse. We are pleased to have this combined empirical and theoretical analysis of *The Discourse of Classified Advertising* as the latest contribution to Oxford Studies in Sociolinguistics.

Edward Finegan

PREFACE

In any urban area, the classified ad columns of the local press reveal a great deal about day-to-day realities. What is it like to live and work here? What does it cost to rent a house? What is the going price for a 1987 Honda Civic? What kind of jobs are available, if any? How do parents find a math tutor for a recalcitrant schoolchild? Do lonely hearts search for partners independently, or are deals still struck between families? For the visitor, the wealth of spontaneous information available in the classified ads has no match even in the best researched travel book, to say nothing of that ultimate advertising concept, the in-flight magazine.

Yet, to the casual observer and the student of advertising alike, the classified ad columns are unobtrusive, unfancied, and mostly taken for granted. Textbooks on the language of advertising typically cover the subject in a few lines, if they mention it at all. Future professional advertisers hone their skills on display advertising and of course on television commercials. Though a few telephone sales executives may earn a commission from encouraging customers to stretch out their texts, few look forward to a challenging career in classified advertising.

The classified ads play a major part in keeping the commercial press alive, since few modern newspapers cover their costs from their cover price alone. Classified ads provide newspapers with a varied and dependable income. Although costs to individual advertisers are low, the aggregate benefit to the newspaper can be vast—so much so that newspapers threatened with a new entrant in the marketplace will not hesitate to protect what is often a local monopoly on classified advertising through expensive advertising campaigns, using TV glamorous commercials to glamorize unglamorous ads if necessary.

So far, the economic benefit of classified advertising to contemporary journalism and its potential for casting light on the social realities of life in a modern city have not been matched by much interest on the part of linguists in general and of discourse analysts in particular. This is curious, if only because access to primary sources is easy, often free, and only limited by the analyst's ability to handle the wealth of material available. For the benefit of analysts of classified advertising, linguistic data grow abundantly in recycling bins, second only in convenience to the intuitional variety, though more reliable as a representation of the human potential for making language mean.

But much more important is that these data have the potential to reveal a great deal about the nature of language, its structure and its use. Earlier research has shown that humans appear to be endowed with the ability to limit the complexities of the language they use to the perceived ability of their interlocutors. Moreover, whenever language is kept simple, to make communication possible with an infant or a foreign visitor, for example, humans appear to rely quite spontaneously on a common core of linguistic strategies which keep linguistic form manageable for all concerned. While this has been widely documented for varieties such as Baby Talk or pidgins, one of the aims of this book is to discover whether similar strategies are also invoked when the texts of classified ads are produced under different constraints such as severe limitations on the space available. Thus the study of classified advertising has the potential to reveal both similarities and differences across a range of simple varieties as well as in the relationship between features of linguistic simplicity and communicative function. This inquiry meant that three major steps had to be taken.

The first is to arrive at a thorough description of the discourse of classified advertising, and a substantial part of this book is devoted to an exploration of what makes this variety distinctive. Just as the language of headlines or of academic note-taking, for example, exhibits a particular set of idiosyncracies, classified ads immediately strike the reader as written in a way which would not be suitable for any other purpose in any other context. Ultimately, the cataloguing of the particular idiosyncracies of the language of classified advertising must be as comprehensive as that of more familiar varieties such as pidgins or standard written English. As many of these idiosyncracies are to be found at the micro-level, that is, in the way in which language is structured over relatively short segments, the descriptive part of this book provides a thorough account of what might be called the syntax of classified ads.

But because few situations of use are ever altogether novel, language in use is unlikely to consist of entirely original combinations and patterns. Since this is as true of the discourse of classified advertising as of any other language variety, a second area of investigation concerns the presence in classified ads of items borrowed from previous discourse and inserted whole into a text. These items can be as short as a three-letter acronym or as long as an entire ad. In addition, recycling and conventionalization can affect the way in which the major semantic components of an ad are sequenced. That is, what is considered important must somehow be highlighted in the text and the appropriate lexico-grammatical strategies must be selected to make these semantic highlights clear to readers. Against a background of formulaic repetition, conventionalized patterns, once set up, can be exploited and departed from to varying degrees of creativity over relatively long stretches of discourse. Whereas previous studies have shown this process at work in the discourse of display advertising and television commercials, it remains to be documented in classified advertising.

Finally, a major aim of the book is to test the assumption that the idiosyncratic form of classified ads is primarily the result of the compression caused by tight spatial constraints. Since few phenomenon can ever be ascribed to a single cause, it is important to investigate whether the linguistic form of classified ads may have wider functional correlates. Here, this involves quantiyfing the presence in these texts of a range of syntactic components, and comparing their distribution across different ad types. If this distribution turns out to be roughly constant despite major differences in content and in communicative purpose between these ad types, then spatial constraints must be assumed to be the dominant factor shaping classified ads. If on the other hand the syntactic characteristics of these texts are found to vary systematically across ad types, then the correlates of that variation will need to be uncovered and a functional explanation offered. In this sense, this book is also a study of register variation.

As always, this kind of book is very much the product of a collaborative effort. Special gratitude is due to Ed Finegan for his repeated interventions in what has been a long process. As chair of my Ph.D. committee, he guided me throughout the early stages of this enterprise with clear directions disguised as gentle hints. As Series Editor for the Oxford Studies in Sociolinguistics series, he motivated me to rethink, polish up, and submit a manuscript when, after three years of close observation, I thought I could not look another classified ad in the eye. He also showed his discernment by selecting two reviewers who contributed a wealth of helpful comments and suggestions. Where I may have let all three down is by not following up on their collective advice more diligently.

A significant part was also played by Robert B. Kaplan, who encouraged me to write early in my graduate career, and whose generous support helped dispel much self-doubt. At the publication stage, Cynthia A. Read, Senior Editor at Oxford University Press, helped to get the project off the ground, and Cynthia L. Garver showed considerable expertise and professionalism in copy-editing the manuscript.

Of course, none of this would have been possible without the myriad of anonymous language users in the Los Angeles area who, by advertising in the *Recycler* and the *LA Weekly* newspapers, unwittingly contributed the raw material to this study. Although I assume most will never get to recognize their compositions in these pages, I hope their endeavors were as rewarding to them as they have been to me and that cars were bought and sold, apartments rented, job offers filled, and romantic partnerships formed to the satisfaction of all concerned.

I am also indebted to my undergraduate students of discourse analysis in the Department of English at City University of Hong Kong who, by demanding weekly clarifications on the connection between language purpose and language form, forced me to work at clarifying it to myself first.

Posthumous gratitude is due to Claudio Monteverdi, Henry Purcell, and François Couperin for setting the words to music.

Finally, no one played a greater part in helping to bring this project to fruition than Min-Kyong Ju. Although her backing took many forms, her most important contributions were her understanding of the vicissitudes of the writing process and her tolerance of its detrimental effect on the quality of her life. This is a better book for her input and her support.

As for its remaining flaws, I am to blame entirely.

Los Angeles P. B.
November 1995

CONTENTS

1 Theoretical issues, 3
    Linguistic simplicity and register variation, 6
    Linguistic simplicity and linguistic theory, 8
    Linguistic simplicity and the parameters of discourse, 11
    Linguistic simplicity and innateness, 19
    Register studies, linguistic simplicity, and classified ads register, 20
    Aims and structure of the book, 21

2 Situating the corpus, 23
    The language of advertising and classified ads register, 23
    Source and nature of the corpus, 31
    Representativeness of the corpus, 36

3 Syntactic elaboration, 39
    Characteristics of syntactic elaboration in classified ads register, 41
    Definite articles, 41
    Indefinite articles, 45
    Pronouns, 49
    Do auxiliaries, 52
    Modals, 54
    Negatives, 57
    Be copulas, 59
    Prepositions, 63
    Relativization, 66
    Lexical compounds, 70
    Coordination, 72
    Subordination, 77
    Adjectival and nominal chains, 79

Economy language and ambiguity, 81
Classified ads register and syntactic elaboration, 84
Summary, 87

4 Conventionalization, 90
Idiomatic sequences, 93
Collocation, 97
Lexical collocation, 97
Structural collocation, 108
Conventionalization and discourse structure, 120
Auto ads, 121
Apartment ads, 124
Job ads, 125
Personal ads, 128
Summary, 130

5 Functional variation, 132
Cross-category analysis of features, 134
Definite articles, 134
Indefinite articles, 137
First and second person pronouns, 137
Relative pronouns, 138
Be copulas, 138
Prepositions, 139
Patterns of distribution, 139
Functional analysis, 143
Definite articles, 144
Indefinite articles, 146
First and second person pronouns, 148
Relative pronouns, 149
Be copulas, 152
Prepositions, 154
Discussion and implications, 156

6 Classified advertising in its linguistic context, 160
Toward a multifunctional model of linguistic simplicity, 161
Description, 161
Processing, 166

Linguistic simplicity and grammatical theory, 170
Suggestions for further research, 173

Appendix A Summary of features of linguistic simplification, 177

Appendix B Corpus selection criteria, 178

Appendix C Glossary of abbreviations, 180

Appendix D Test of editorial interference in *Recycler* ads, 184

Notes, 187

References, 193

Index, 204

The Discourse
of Classified Advertising

1

Theoretical issues

If asked to evaluate the relative degrees of linguistic simplicity of, say, a conversation between an adult and a child on the one hand and a legal document on the other, most people would probably and consistently rate the former as simpler than the latter. When it comes to language use, teachers and caregivers, airline pilots and market traders all take it for granted that producing and understanding simple, easily accessible language is a routine aspect of communication, whether the ability to do this comes instinctively or has to be acquired through training.

But this does not mean that a principled account of linguistic simplicity, in comprehension or in production, is so readily available. Halliday (1989) convincingly shows that in formal, technical writing, actions and processes are often encoded as nouns instead of verbs, a writing strategy known as *nominalization*. This allows the writer to dispense with many of the conjunctions normally needed to encode related ideas as related clauses and sentences. It leads to a lower frequency of coordination and subordination and therefore to simpler syntactic structure. But the resulting high density of nouns may simultaneously make processing more arduous. In contrast, Schleppegrell (1992) shows that greater levels of coordination should not imply greater linguistic complexity because coordinating clauses can operate both as expressions of relatedness in discourse and as expansions of previous discourse. This is especially true in spoken language, in which frequent conjunctions such as *and* or *so* can act as agents of clarification and therefore simplification. This follows a line of argument pursued earlier by Shuy & Larkin (1978), who claimed that deliberate attempts at simplification could in fact lead to greater difficulties in comprehension and that many of the simplifying efforts of public discourse undertaken in the United States under the heading of "Plain English" were based on a muddled view of simplicity. A restricted lexical and syntactic inventory may make encoding easier, Shuy & Larkin argued, but it can obscure semantic intentions by depriving decoders of the benefits of redundancy. Conversely, specialized jargon, often decried as a marker of elitism or even of intentional obfuscation, can in fact be a simplifying factor because it can minimize the need for elaborate circumlocutions, provided of course that it is used appropriately.

Generally speaking, linguistic simplicity—to the extent that it can be correlated with successful communication—depends in part on encoders making linguistic choices that are appropriate to the context and on decoders being aware of the encoder's expectations in each context. As Shuy & Larkin (1978) argue, shorter words may tend to be more frequent and therefore more familiar, in English at least. But if they are used inappropriately, they will not be simpler than longer, less familiar words that are used appropriately. In addition, all language use—but especially face-to-face interaction—forces encoders to make a myriad of assumptions about what decoders need to be told. Corners are cut, shared knowledge is merely evoked, and the resulting surface organization of a text can never be a direct map of its intended meaning. If comprehension is so heavily dependent on inferencing, an account of linguistic simplicity cannot therefore be reduced to a correlation between the degree of syntactic elaboration and transparency. Thus Shuy & Larkin's rejection of the indiscriminate application of formulaic strategies of simplification regardless of circumstances remains valid today.

To be sure, any attempt to characterize linguistic simplicity should beware of ironclad definitions and assumptions of single causes. The fact that a given linguistic form appears in two different systems does not have to stem from a common motivation. Although language learners may find the lack of one-to-one mapping between form and function problematic at first, no competent language user has any difficulty accepting polysemy, for example, or the fact that a given syntactic form may be required to perform several communicative functions, as in imperatives commonly encoding invitations or instructions, in addition to orders. Nor should one expect a given linguistic form to strike the user as equally simple or equally complex in different contexts, in comprehension and in production. For example, among the factors that determine how simple a feature appears to a pidgin user are naturalness, frequency, and an array of pragmatic and contextual considerations (Mühlhaüsler, 1986). As a result, a model of linguistic simplicity must be a multidimensional one, which should take into account relations between different measures of complexity, as well as between text types defined by their component clusters of linguistic features, in comprehension and in production (Finegan & Biber, 1986; Biber, 1992). Ultimately, an account of linguistic simplicity must also imply a psycholinguistic approach, which should measure simplicity in terms of greater speed and accuracy of processing and production. A recent example of this type of work is Kemper et al. (1993), which finds a correlation between the reading comprehension of older adults to the semantic density and the syntactic complexity of their reading materials.

However, before we can gain a better understanding of some of the psycholinguistic correlates of linguistic simplicity and of the formal characteristics of simple language, two fundamentals need to be spelled out. First, analysts should guard against the presupposition that there is a fully grammatical underlying model from which simpler—and somehow more marginal—varieties are derived. It is to guard against this danger that I use the term *simple* throughout this book in preference to the more widely used label *simplified*. Second, there is a need for a much wider range of descriptive studies of specific simple varieties, which should reveal differences across these varieties in patterns of simplicity, as well as in the relationship between features of linguistic simplicity and communicative function. As Ferguson writes, the study of simple registers has the potential to shed light not only on the notion of linguistic simplicity but also on "the fundamental role of situational variation in the characterization of language structure" (1982, p. 63). In brief, before one makes psycholinguistic investigations of how language comes to be perceived as more or less simple, one's study of simplicity must be essentially descriptive. That is, language form should be thoroughly described and systematic variation should be related to the specific circumstances of use of each variety across a range of simple registers. In this sense, a study of linguistic simplicity must be a study of register variation.

Linguistic simplicity and register variation

Language form varies, among other reasons, because language itself is capable of much more than performing a propositional role—that is, simply naming topics and predicating something of them. Among other nonpropositional functions of language are displaying deference, controlling the interaction, persuading, comforting, antagonizing, intimidating, impressing, and many more. Variation thus reflects in part the range of functional and interpersonal factors that can be loaded onto propositional content. Linguistic form is also shaped by different conditions of production, transmission, and reception. For example, having to produce largely unplanned language in face-to-face interaction will result in a language form that is substantially different from that of a carefully edited written message. This occurs because more ample planning time allows for greater use of complex sentences, while more ample processing time allows for a higher frequency of heavy modification of nouns by strings of adjectives. For the analyst, it is the consistent matching of clusters of linguistic features with specific language use that constitutes a *register* (Halliday & Hasan, 1989). In other words, systematic differences between, say, conversational and literary production can be seen in evolutionary terms as linguistic adaptation to the different conditions under which each register typically operates (Pawley & Syder, 1983a). That is, language users will evolve consistent, often conventionalized strategies for dealing with recurring situations (Chafe, 1987; Ferguson, 1994). So fundamental is the systematic link between form and function that recognition of this relationship by infants is at the heart of the process of becoming a competent member of a society (Ochs & Schieffelin, 1984) and may well precede the vocalizations normally deemed to represent the beginnings of language (Ferguson, 1982).

If, as Ferguson writes, "a communication situation that recurs regularly in a society . . . will tend over time to develop identifying markers of language structure and language use, different from the language of other communication situations" (1994, p. 20), detailed descriptions of the functional parameters of a discourse are essential to our understanding of why specific linguistic features occur as and when they do. Admittedly, situation (the context of utterance) and function (what role language is meant to play within that context and how it is meant to influence it) cannot easily be separated. But given that situations obviously exist independently from any linguistic responses that they may or may not generate, I use the term *functional* throughout this book in preference to the more passive-sounding *situational*.

Although the relationship between form and function is widely acknowledged to be the key to discourse studies, the notion of register might gain from being conceptualized more in correlational than in deterministic terms. That is, a register might be described as a cluster of features having a greater than random tendency to co-occur in a given context (Halliday, 1991). To quote Halliday directly, "just as we define regions of the globe by reference to their weather patterns, so . . . we can define registers by references to their grammatical probabilities: register variation is the resetting of the probabilities in the grammar . . . within the values defined by the system type" (p. 38). This approach challenges the assumption of a qualitative gap between *competence* and *performance*, between *system* (the grammar) and *token* (each actual example), that is central to a generative perspective on language. Instead, far from dismissing corpus studies as having little to contribute toward an understanding of language, a probabilistic approach to register variation sees that the concept of frequency is central to linguistic analysis because it is the primary indicator of the limits of variation—that is, of the very boundaries of one register and neighboring registers.

In a widely accepted definition, Halliday & Hasan characterize registers as "varieties according to use," in contrast to dialects, which can be described as "varieties according to user" (1989, p. 41). Further distinctions also need to be made with two related terms. One of these is *genre*, which has traditionally carried literary rather than linguistic connotations. Within discourse analysis, the term has more recently referred to texts commonly used by a narrowly defined set of professionals and shaped by a common pattern of discourse structure (see, for example, Swales, 1990; Bhatia, 1993; Ferguson, 1994). However, the constituent texts of a genre may share only superficial, sometimes merely visual, similarities. For example, most texts within the genre of *letters* tend to share many of their surface characteristics. Yet a detailed analysis of their linguistic features will reveal fundamental differences between, say, business and personal letters. Whereas business letters make greater use of nominalizations and avoid short forms for auxiliaries, the reverse is true of personal letters. A second notion to be contrasted with the term *register* is that of *text type*, which relies on the co-occurrence of linguistic features not covered by the labels *register* or *genre* (Biber, 1988). For example, both conversation and personal letters may be seen as one text type cutting across two genres because they share—albeit for independent reasons—a preference for placing adjectives in predicative position, as in *the food is tasty*, as opposed to attributive use, as in *tasty food*. Most probably, the preference of speakers in face-to-face interaction for following the unmarked pattern of topic (*food*) before comment (*tasty*) can be explained by processing difficulties. But this constraint does not apply to writers of personal letters, who have the benefit of more ample planning time and probably choose wordings borrowed from face-to-face interaction in order to index interactional involvement—to make their writing look more like speech, in other words.

In the broadest sense, the label *register* can apply to a language variety defined by a single functional characteristic, for example, spoken language (Besnier, 1986). In a narrow sense, a register can also be identified on the basis of a restricted set of features correlating with a unique condition of use that offers little or no room for creativity, as in the narrowly focused and highly regulated register of air traffic (Fitzpatrick, Bachenko, & Hindle, 1986; Robertson, 1987). Although in practice many registers probably fall halfway between the two extremes, it is toward the narrow end of this characterization that many descriptions of simple registers are to be found. This includes the register of classified advertising in American English, henceforth here called the *classified ads register* (CAR), which is the central focus of this book.

Linguistic simplicity and linguistic theory

I have already argued that a range of functional parameters play a key part in shaping linguistic form. Among these are opportunities for planning and the availability of feedback, as well as differences in interlocutor status and the need to indicate affect and stance. Messages also need to be couched in terms appropriate to the linguistic ability of the interlocutors, all within the temporal or spatial constraints of each situation. From this perspective, the label *simple register* may be applied to language produced under conditions in which one or more constraints require that linguistic form be kept well short of the degree of syntactic elaboration commonly associated with the written form. At one level at least, simple language is thus *maximally appropriate discourse*. That is, it offers the best fit of all possible linguistic responses to specific functional demands within the limits of what both the encoder and the decoder can jointly handle.

This is not to say that language users must start with syntactically elaborated language consisting of sentences fully acceptable to grammarians, which is then simplified—consciously or otherwise— to fit the demands of the interaction. In other words, there is no a priori reason to suppose—despite, as I have already argued, what is suggested by the conventional application of the term *simplified* to simple registers—that all simple language is underpinned by elaborated form from which simpler texts are derived through the deletion of redundant material. To be sure, early generative assumptions of linguistic production as the outcome of syntactic transformations no longer need to be challenged. Yet their influence still permeates research on linguistic simplicity, much of which appears to presuppose the existence, prior to the simplification that involves deletion, of the kind of sentences found in the formal, mostly written language, on which generative linguists typically draw for their intuitions of grammaticality. As Mühlhaüsler (1986) points out, this occurs despite the fact that assumptions of a clear correspondence between grammatical descriptions and mental processes, and a tradition of referring to both under the single label of *grammar*, can be unhelpful or even misleading. Given the enduring influence of the generative paradigm, however, it is not surprising to find it that influenced many early studies of simplicity and gave rise to a preoccupation with the place of "deviant" linguistic phenomena (Ferguson, 1977, p. 209) within the unified system envisaged by generative linguists.[1]

The labeling of some varieties of discourse as simplified can thus be linked to the widespread assumption that all language must be related, regardless of functional parameters, to a single standard, typically the grammar of formal written language (henceforth, the *literary grammar*).[2] From this perspective, therefore, the study of linguistic simplicity consists of the relatively easy task of measuring differences between that standard and the simple register under investigation. However, this ignores the fact that formal written registers are no more free of constraints than are any other registers (Chafe, 1980, 1985, 1986; Pawley & Syder, 1983a, 1983b; Biber, 1988, 1994). Instead, formal written language is the way it is because it, too, is shaped by specific circumstances of use. Only the combined forces of scholastic tradition and current paradigms explain its continued high status within linguistics.

Another approach consists of analyzing simplicity in terms of markedness. It could be argued, for example, that simple language should be more natural, or maximally unmarked. It should be more iconic and uniform and should tend to avoid allomorphy and polyfunctionality (Heine, Claudi, & Hünnemeyer, 1991). From this perspective, a correlation might be found between the degree of naturalness—assuming that naturalness can be measured—and neurolinguistic factors, in the sense that "what is natural is . . . easy for the human brain" (p. 119), in comprehension and in production. But as I stated at the outset, there is already among language users at large a widely observed readiness to produce, as well as recognize, appropriately simple language. Among linguists also, there is a large measure of consensus over what the major features of simple language are (Ferguson, 1982). For example, commentators as varied as Meisel (1977), Ferguson & DeBose (1977), Mühlhaüsler (1986), Romaine (1988), Holm (1988), and Todd (1990) all share a view of pidgins that is characterized by minimal syntactic elaboration and minimization of both lexical repertory and semantic complexity. As a result, it is widely accepted that simple registers must entail a severe limitation in the scope of each variety's communicative use. Nowhere is the commonality among simple registers better articulated than in Ferguson's (1982, p. 60) typology of what he sees as the major features of these registers: smaller, generic rather than specific vocabulary; monomorphemic words and paraphrases of complex words; little or no subordination but parataxis; invariant word order; invariant stems with little or no inflection; and absence of copula, pronouns, and function words. (See appendix A for full details of Ferguson's typology.)

Another approach to the classification of simple varieties as described here is to see them in terms of *restrictive* simplification, a label proposed by Meisel (1977, 1983a, 1983b). Meisel contrasts this with *elaborative* simplification, which he defines as a tendency to regularize discrete, ad hoc strategies and forms into a system capable of expanding to the point where it can take on the multiplicity of functions required of a fully fledged language. In this type of simplification, rules acquire greater generality as exceptions are eliminated, paradigmatic gaps are plugged, and the lexicon becomes increasingly grammaticalized (Mühlhaüsler, 1974, 1986; Todd, 1990). This is a process characteristic of the later stages of the transition from pidgin to creole and of the learner's advance toward greater competence in the first and, in Schumann's (1978) view, the second language. More pertinent to the analysis of CAR is a potential contrast between, at one end of a continuum, language that is *elaborated,* in that it tends to meet the syntactic requirements of the literary grammar in full, and, clustering toward the opposite extreme of the continuum, language that might be labeled *restricted,* in that some syntactic features appear to be missing from contexts in which the rules of the literary grammar normally make them obligatory. However, given that throughout this book I choose to make no claim for the centrality of deletion processes in the production and comprehension of simple language, much of the available terminology is found wanting. Thus one of my aims in this book is to suggest more appropriate terminology for some of the concepts central to the study of linguistic simplicity.

Linguistic simplicity and the parameters of discourse

Language handicap

Linguistic restriction

Discourse addressed to speakers with limited competence in the language, typically at the earlier stage of linguistic development, is often characterized by widespread syntactic restriction. In nascent pidgins, where the phenomenon is well documented, this is due to an extreme asymmetry between a speaker's competence in one language and, initially at least, complete ignorance of the other. Here, minimizing syntactic elaboration aims at optimal communication by keeping form at a level of sophistication that encoder and decoder can jointly handle. Major features of these registers include the absence of articles and copulas, a substantial narrowing of the inflectional system, a slower rate of delivery, and the avoidance of false starts and digressions (Hatch, 1983a). Description of this type of discourse in terms of handicap can be traced back to Ferguson (1971), and the label *handicap register* is proposed by Bruthiaux (1993, 1994), without, of course, implying pejorative connotations of substandard competence on the part of any of the interactants.

Prominent among handicap registers is *baby talk* (BT), a term widely used to describe the language used by caregivers when addressing young children, but also covering the speech of infants progressing toward the first language target.[3] Much has been made of the finding that recourse to BT is not universal and that it appears to be considered inappropriate in some cultures (Ochs & Schieffelin, 1984). Yet its spread is sufficiently well documented to permit the generalization that its main function is the transmission not only of elements of the linguistic system itself but also of information regarding sequencing, turn-taking, and feedback strategies (Shatz & Gelman, 1977; Hatch, 1983b), as well as the expression of emotions (Ferguson, 1977). This transmission of information can be achieved by providing listeners with more syntactically elaborated, more adultlike utterances and turns. But what makes this register distinctive is minimal syntactic elaboration (Ferguson & DeBose, 1977) and the almost total absence of the frequent topic shifts and structural readjustments that characterize adult-to-adult speech (Gleitman, Newport, & Gleitman, 1984). Still, interactive elements are very much part of the nature of BT, as evidenced by the systematic relationship that holds between the degree of *babyishness* and the state of the child's linguistic development (Ferguson, 1977). Utterances that go beyond the child's current competence tend to lead to inattention and failure to respond until modified input generates an appropriate response on the part of the child (Snow, 1986). Since there is no a priori reason to believe that similar interactive factors do not also play a part in other simple registers, I propose to investigate in this book their role in shaping CAR texts.

A second major type of simple register is *foreigner talk* (FT), a term used to refer to discourse produced by native speakers of a language who may attempt to facilitate communication by adjusting their speech to the presumed capabilities of a nonnative, adult interlocutor. In addition to a relatively limited didactic role (Fathman, 1977), FT can index both social superiority and empathy or affection (Ferguson & DeBose, 1977). Typically the register relies on amplification of pitch and volume, syntactic expansion, lexical reordering and substitution, and greater use of feedback devices and comprehension checks (Ferguson, 1975). But linguistic simplicity of the restricted kind is also apparent in minimal coordination and inflection, low frequency of function words, and modifications to the speed and length of utterance (Ferguson & DeBose, 1977; Hatch, 1983a). In addition to being constrained by cognitive and interactional factors such as perceived power relations, FT is marked by the conventionalization of features that continue to be recycled, often in literary form, long after their functional justification has ceased to apply (Ferguson, 1975; Mühlhaüsler, 1986). Here, too, it is not likely that the phenomenon of conventionalization affects only FT alone among simple registers, and the possibility that it may have parallels in CAR is an issue I discuss in this book.

At least in its incipient form, a *pidgin* is a restricted system of the handicap type in which extended contact between groups with no common language results in a combination of elements of both parties' languages (Mühlhaüsler, 1986; Holm, 1988; Romaine, 1988; Todd, 1990). There is among analysts a sense that what makes pidgins simple is essentially restriction in syntactic scope. But restriction also affects the size of the lexical inventory in response to the narrow functional scope of the variety, although this is compensated for by an extension of the semantic scope of the restricted inventory. As with FT, much of this restriction can surface in a conventionalized, often derogatory form in literary approximations of the register (Mühlhaüsler, 1986). Thus my earlier characterization of simple registers as maximally appropriate language echoes Romaine (1988), who highlights the relevance of pidgins to the study of all language varieties—including, presumably, simple registers—and argues for the "instant pidgin" nature of all acts of language use created by "the on-going need in all human communicative settings for speakers to negotiate a common set of meanings through the linguistic means available to them" (p. 24). I should stress that handicap registers do not have a monopoly on the use of restrictive strategies. Many of these strategies may be shared with language varieties shaped by different functional circumstances. For example, restrictive strategies such as phonemic or morphological mergers may be common to processes of language acquisition, pidginization, and language death (Dorian, 1981; Schmidt, 1985; Eung-Do Cook, 1989). But whereas a pidgin normally arises out of formal dealings between strangers, a dying language typically serves to reinforce informal, close personal ties among members of a single, small community. Thus, as I mentioned earlier, reliance on common strategies does not mean that both varieties are necessarily closely related phenomena, much less mirror images of each other.

Linguistic elaboration

Just as common reliance on restrictive strategies does not imply common causes, a register of the handicap type will not necessarily consist of restrictive strategies. In her comparison of *judges' clarifications* of defendants' constitutional rights with the written source, Philips (1985) notes that the strategies used by different judges show a remarkable degree of similarity, especially considering that each judge has approached the problem largely independently. She finds that judges typically attempt to make the content of their message more accessible by, for example, transforming original segments such as heavy nominalizations—the products of the dense integration of information characteristic of legal language—into a series of subordinate and relative clauses. The result is a lower level of lexical density and an increase in syntactic complexity simultaneously.

Simple discourse that meets the requirements of the literary grammar is also found in those *didactic texts* that have been manipulated to make them more accessible to first and second language learners or to older adults with reading difficulties. The widely accepted claim is that greater syntactic simplicity and greater accessibility can be achieved by reducing the number of subordinate clauses. This can be seen in recent work such as Cervantes & Gainer (1992), Leow (1993), and Kemper et al. (1993), who all report a correlation between this reduction and higher levels of reading comprehension, although Schleppegrell (1992) offers interesting counterevidence. Simplicity for didactic purposes can also result from attempts to make intratextual relationships more evident through the increased use of cohesive devices and to make patterns of information ordering such as topic/comment sequencing conform to the expectations of linguistically handicapped readers, especially second language learners (Lautamatti, 1987).

Language economy

Linguistic restriction

Simple registers can also involve interlocutors constrained not by limited linguistic competence but by a variety of spatial or temporal factors. These limitations on the time or space available for encoding messages can result in what Halliday calls the "economy grammar" of "display languages" such as newspaper headlines (1967, p. 11). Other labels attached to these registers are "little" (Halliday, 1985, p. 372) and "compressed" (Sinclair, 1988, p. 130). Since the fulfillment of a communicative purpose is here heavily dependent on economy of expression, these varieties can be gathered under the label of *economy register* (Bruthiaux, 1993, 1994). It is typically assumed that the spatial and temporal constraints under which these registers operate force encoders to excise redundant information, with a concomitant loss of explicitness. In this view, spatial constraints boil language down to the bare essentials of linguistic structure: these registers offer few stylistic options, and they emphasize propositional content at the expense of the expression of affect or stance. I examine these assumptions critically throughout this book in the light of evidence from CAR.

Like handicap registers, economy registers exhibit many of the features listed in Ferguson's (1982) typology. Unlike handicap registers, they do not typically entail loss of referential power, although some specialization in subject matter is normally involved. Users of economy registers assume that aiming for maximally appropriate—and maximally simple—language choices will not create insurmountable difficulties for decoders. With respect to classified ads, for example, anecdotal evidence suggests that once a few common code words and abbreviations have been learned, decoding does not typically suffer as a result of compression. Whether it does or does not is a point worthy of separate investigation of a psycholinguistic nature. However, this is an undertaking that lies outside the scope of this book.

Waiting to be researched are economy registers such as telephone messages, personal diaries, and, briefly noted by Ferguson (1971), the language of instructions printed on packaging, in which convention as much as lack of space can lead to limited syntactic elaboration. Best known among economy registers is probably the compressed language of newspaper headlines, labeled *headlinese* by Mårdh (1980). In this register also, limited elaboration is probably at least as conventional as it is spatial, and the register depends for its effectiveness on balancing the pressure for economy with the fact that meaning needs to be recoverable despite a paucity of contextual clues. While pressure for economy can result in heavily modified nominal groups, simplicity can be seen in the frequent omission of articles, auxiliaries, and copulas from contexts in which the literary grammar would regard such features as obligatory.

Academic *note-taking* (NT) offers another opportunity to study simplicity, this time by comparing a restricted—or, as it might quite properly be called, reduced—output (students' lecture notes) with its source (the live lecture) (Janda, 1985). As in BT, FT, pidgins, and headlinese, restriction is apparent in the frequent omission from NT texts of many function words such as articles, copulas, pronouns, and auxiliaries. But as I stressed earlier, the presence of a feature in two or more registers does not imply a single motivation or a single set of functional characteristics. Whereas, for example, the omission of personal pronouns in BT and FT might be due to the kind of cognitive difficulties generally observed in language acquisition, in NT this feature may reflect the fact that personal pronouns are simply absent from the source. Moreover, NT does not exhibit some of the features commonly found in BT and FT, such as a generalized absence of tense inflections and the omission of auxiliaries in negative constructions. Finally the restrictive (and reductive) strategies of NT may also surface even when there is sufficient time to write the source material in full. While this may be due to economy of effort, it is difficult to determine at which point what began as an ad hoc strategy became a routinized part of a writer's style. What is needed, therefore, is a multifunctional model of these and other constituents of linguistic simplicity.

The final example of a register in which the need for economy results in linguistic restriction is *sports announcer talk* (SAT). Studied by Ferguson (1983), Ghadessy (1988), and Romaine (1994), it is a live monolog (or sometimes dialog) directed at an unknown, heterogeneous, and unseen audience that provides no feedback. It is constrained by a requirement for economy due essentially to the lack of planning time. The omission of material obligatory in the literary grammar is common in frequency but limited in type. Most pervasive of this phenomenon is the omission of pronouns, which can usually be reconstructed on the basis of contextual information, although no source is available for comparison. Other distinctive features of the register include the frequent use of inversions of subject noun phrases and verb phrases and heavy modification of noun phrases, often by means of elaborate relativization and multiple embeddings. Given the on-line pressures that shape the register, skillful handling of these features must rely in part on repeated practice, probably leading to a degree of conventionalization.

Linguistic elaboration

Although it does not come naturally to mind in discussions of simple registers, poetry—at least in classical form—is one type of language in which the pressures for economy must be reconciled with the demands of the literary grammar, as well as demands of the various prosodic rules that differentiate one type or poem from another. Space is one of a number of constraints often imposed on the form, nowhere more so than in the extensively analyzed *sonnet* (Friedrich, 1988) and especially the *limerick*, which aims to create, sustain, and resolve dramatic tension within strict metrical rules over a very short span (Baring-Gould, 1967). Both forms share a substantial number of characteristics with headlinese as well as CAR, including the need to operate within rigid spatial constraints, opportunities for careful planning, and the control exercised by a powerful set of conventions. However, the output consistently conforms to—and often surpasses— the requirements of the literary grammar, and the syntactic restriction visible in other simple registers in the form of missing copulas, auxiliaries, or pronouns is unacceptable.

Social distancing

Following Ferguson (1985), a review of simple registers must include registers that aim for a degree of simplicity as a tool for social distancing. Under the labels *mother-in-law* (Dixon, 1971) and *avoidance* (Haviland, 1979), these registers, described mostly in research among native Australian communities, constitute a linguistic index of social relationships within a society. They consist of a highly codified vocabulary of respect toward relatives and of a system of rules about what words, if any, may be substituted for taboo terms. Other features are restricted verb morphology and the slower and softer pronunciation of certain words in the register-changing presence of a taboo relative. An avoidance register can also be supplemented by body language that aims to minimize interaction, especially among community members with little competence in the register.

With a decreasing number of young people acquiring competence in these registers, they now tend to mark group solidarity among those who use them (the old) as opposed to those who do not (the young). But they also remain of interest to the analyst because the phenomenon may have parallels in other registers such as BT, FT, or pidgins, in which even body language may form an integral part of linguistic simplicity in the sense that it offers a vital set of extralinguistic clues for the benefit of the addressee. Indeed, there is no obvious reason why descriptions of the phenomenon should be restricted to the native Australian context. Most probably, equally abrupt changes in pitch or volume on emotionally charged or taboo words could be linked to the presence of register-changing individuals in specific environments across a much wider range of societies and situations.

Linguistic simplicity and innateness

Much of the research devoted to linguistic simplicity in the last two decades has in some way addressed the possibility that simple registers may stem partly from the operation of a human—and possibly innate—capacity for producing and understanding simple language. The suggestion is that widely observed characteristics of linguistic simplicity, such as the relative rarity of function words and morphological endings or restriction in the phonological inventory, may be part of a universal predisposition to recognize and, if necessary, return to certain basic properties of language that were at the core of the initial acquisition process. Unmarked for any particular language, these strategies may be part of the universal foundation of linguistic competence and thus require no special learning (Samarin, 1971; Ferguson, 1971, 1975, 1982).

Much of the initial justification for hypothesizing an innate capacity for keeping language simple rests in studies of pidginization. The claim is that the striking number of characteristics shared by pidgins is a surface manifestation of universal patterns of linguistic behavior appropriate to identical situations (Mühlhaüsler, 1986; Holm, 1988; Romaine, 1988; Todd, 1990). Worldwide parallels across pidgins cannot be explained merely by attribution to compromises achieved through mutual imitation. What is proposed instead is that human beings may be innately capable of systematically keeping their production free of whatever syntactic and other refinements may stand in the way of successful communication. From this perspective, the pressure to keep language simple in order to communicate with a linguistically handicapped interlocutor or to save time or space may encourage the language user to fall back on an unmarked linguistic core common to all simple varieties.

This is not to say that speakers will universally tend toward an equal degree of simplicity in identical situations. In actual performance, the social context may well determine when simplicity is appropriate and when it is not. Ochs & Schieffelin (1984), for example, show that whereas Samoan adults accommodate to foreigners through FT, they do not seem to use BT when acting as caregivers. However, provided a society sanctions recourse to simple discourse, speakers may be innately equipped with the ability to employ it effortlessly, an ability that may go some way toward explaining the high degree of resemblance noted by Ferguson (1982) across simple registers.

However, there can be little doubt that many of the appropriate modes of expression for each communicative situation must to some extent be learned through imitation.[4] Thus, whatever role possibly innate mechanisms may play in shaping simple language, a truly comprehensive account of linguistic simplicity will also need to consider the extent of conventionalization in language use. But while learned and imitative behavior may help explain in part the linguistic form of classified ads, it does not account for the striking similarities that mark simple registers, including CAR. Thus I will need to test the claim that a possibly innate capacity for producing simple language may play a major part in shaping CAR texts. I will do this by studying the effect of narrow spatial constraints on the frequency in CAR of some of the features noted by Ferguson (1982) for their generalized rarity in simple registers.

Register studies, linguistic simplicity, and classified ads register

In their extensive review of research into register variation, Atkinson & Biber (1994) note that synchronic, single-register analysis is the most prototypical approach. Until relatively recently this research was largely limited to the description of lexical and syntactic features of selected, and mostly written, registers (Atkinson, 1991). Ervin-Tripp (1972) and Ferguson & DeBose (1977) represent early attempts to make the assignment of the label *register* to a language variety dependent on the identification of clusters of features that correlate consistently with specific conditions of use. More recently, sophisticated statistical tools have been applied to large corpora, most notably in the work of Biber (1988, 1994). This allows the labeling of registers to be determined by patterns of co-occurrence of linguistic features as determined by powerful computational tools. It also contrasts with more conventional work—including this study of classified ads—which identifies a register in terms of its conventional appearance before examining any possible interaction between its functional parameters and linguistic form.[5] Thus both approaches remain essentially descriptive, a label that Ferguson sees as an advantage since descriptive studies "may be more constructive contributions to the development of sociolinguistics than elaborate but premature attempts at theory" (1983, p. 13).

Aims and structure of the book

Since CAR texts are produced under controlled and broadly uniform conditions, a study of this register offers a chance to add a principled description to a limited inventory of detailed register studies. One of my aims in this book is thus to broaden current perceptions of linguistic simplicity by providing an extensive description of a register that is little researched despite being widely experienced by language users at large. To this end, I describe the occurrence and distribution of a number of features of syntactic elaboration whose absence is widely assumed to characterize simple texts. To satisfy my descriptive purpose, I also survey the extent of conventionalization as it affects abbreviations and specialized codes, as well as the sequencing of semantic components, and the recycling of familiar patterns and segments.

A more narrowly focused aim is to test the assumption that the omission of nonessential items results essentially from the compression caused by spatial constraints. I do this by first comparing the frequency of a number of features that appear to give CAR its distinctive form with their frequency across a wider range of texts. The next step is to correlate that frequency with spatial constraints. Since these are largely constant, their effect should be felt uniformly across different ad categories. However, if levels of elaboration as measured by the frequency of a set of syntactic features such as function words are found to vary across ad categories, other correlates of that variation will need to be uncovered and a functional explanation offered.

Following this introductory chapter, I devote chapter 2 to a detailed discussion of my claim that CAR is a suitable candidate for the type of analysis I have just outlined. I review previous literature on the language of simple registers, of advertising in general and of classified advertising in particular. I also detail the procedures followed in assembling a corpus of classified ads suitable for analysis. In chapter 3, I examine the role played in the construction of CAR texts by a selection of syntactic and discoursal features, and I note that whereas some of the features found in CAR are shared with several simpler registers, others are specific to this register. I consider the extent to which these features conform to the requirements of the literary grammar that underpins formal, typically written registers. In chapter 4, I focus on the frequency and distribution of conventionalized register markers such as abbreviations. After also examining the role played by prefabricated segments, I present a picture of CAR as the product not so much of a reduction from syntactically elaborated underlying form but of a partial but maximally appropriate syntactic elaboration. In chapter 5, I note that identical spatial constraints do not in fact have a uniform effect on CAR texts, and I consider some of the functional factors that might account for this pattern of variation. In the closing chapter, I examine the validity of claims for a cross-linguistic and possibly innate sense of what constitutes linguistic simplicity, and I challenge the view that the process of making language simple consists essentially of top-down deletion from more elaborated underlying forms. I also consider the impact of conventionalized and prefabricated segments on the writing and reading of CAR texts. I discuss some of the theoretical assumptions that frame the study of language in context, and of register variation in particular, in the light of findings from this study of CAR. Finally, I outline some implications of this discussion for further research.

2

Situating the corpus

The language of advertising and classified ads register

Initially at least, CAR is readily recognizable as a register in the sense that the frequency of function words or the reliance on abbreviations tends to correlate with specific functional parameters. These include the presentation of narrowly focused information in texts produced under largely uniform spatial constraints and normally benefiting from ample planning time. CAR also qualifies as a simple register in that it typically falls short—sometimes dramatically so—of the degree of elaboration usually associated with written language.

Another major reason for regarding CAR as especially suitable for the analysis of register variation is that it is produced in naturalistic conditions under consistently tight constraints, which should factor out many social and individual variables. One of the major characteristics of CAR is that it is not typically constrained by linguistic handicaps on the part of either the encoder or the decoder. It is true that some types of classified ads can be decoded successfully by less than fully competent readers such as immigrants in search of jobs or accommodation, provided they have acquired basic scanning skills and some knowledge of key codes and abbreviations. Similarly, auto ads may be scanned solely to determine the value of an auto the reader may wish to sell, and personals may be read out of sheer curiosity or simply for their entertainment value. But it is not likely that actual ad writers will be motivated to adjust their output to the needs of peripheral segments of their potential readership or to the marginal uses that may be made of their text.

The language of advertising is by definition nonreciprocal (Lakoff, 1982), and CAR is no exception. Typically, classified ads aim at a linguistically competent but unknown reader who chooses to read but cannot coconstruct text through immediate feedback. It is also different from an economy register such as *headlinese*, in which the writer can risk (and often aims for) a degree of opacity that will normally be disambiguated in the article itself (Crystal & Davy, 1969). Since the medium offers no second chance for clarification, the message of each ad must be explanatory. And because the format does not normally permit saliency for specific ads without considerable additional expense, it must also be attention grabbing, especially since obviously persuasive elements—such as catchy visuals—tend to be absent from these texts and very little can be done to induce a prospective public to read them (Vestergaard & Schrøder, 1985). Meanwhile, writers are constrained by stringent and uniform parameters, just as the note-taker with no shorthand skills is constrained temporally. In addition, the texts of classified ads are not normally constrained by pressure for on-line production, thus allowing writers considerable scope for editing. It is true that some variation may exist in the degree of editorial interference by newspaper employees who accept classified ads over the phone. But whatever the degree of coconstruction of these texts, they remain largely free of the influence exerted by the need for on-line production and lack of planning time, which can be said to be largely responsible for the linguistic form of face-to-face interactions, for example. Finally, editorial policy places further constraints on what and how much may be written. Although content and form vary across publications, both are likely to be highly consistent within each newspaper.

Studies of the discourse of advertising with a linguistic focus remain relatively rare. In the sense that they constitute departures from the study of more elaborated linguistic form, they are all indebted, directly or indirectly, to Straumann's (1935) pioneering work on the unusual syntax of telegrams and headlines, for which he coined the term *block language*. Among a range of linguistic features that made these two simple varieties distinct, Straumann noted a generalized absence of articles, a predominance of nouns and nominal groups and a concomitant rarity of verbs, and frequent syntactic disjunction. But he did not speculate much on the possible functional causes of these features.

Crystal & Davy (1969) follow in Straumann's footsteps in that their analysis of the language of newspaper reporting is primarily a taxonomy of major linguistic features found in just two contrastive news articles on the same topic but published by two different newspapers. Crystal & Davy go over much the same ground as Straumann, including the simple syntax of headlines. But they also consider reference, information structure, and visual elements such as paragraphing and punctuation. In this they foreshadow more recent work in text linguistics such as Biber's (1988) computational analysis in that they assume a direct link between a given set of linguistics characteristics and the functional circumstances of newspaper reporting. But in keeping with the best-informed practice of the time, they base their assessment of what constitutes journalistic language—or, as they call it, *journalese*—only on their own estimate of the appropriate level of analysis. At a more general level, they argue, a description of journalistic English would be so sweeping as to include most written communication. At a more restrictive level, the exercise would degenerate into endless subclassifying, with little or no explanatory power. This contrasts with modern computational approaches, which permit the identification of broad text types on the basis not of the analyst's intuition about where categorical boundaries may lie but of clusters of linguistic features in very large corpora.

In much the same tradition but much more narrowly focused is Mårdh's (1980) analysis of the language of headlines in two British newspapers from opposite ends of the spectrum, from low-brow to high-brow. In addition to providing a comprehensive review of previous studies of the syntax of *headlinese*, Mårdh describes in some detail the use made in headlines of familiar linguistic features such as nouns and nominal groups, articles, and verbs. She also considers the number and length of words, the number and type of clauses, and the number of modifiers in noun phrases. In addition, she discusses—but does not propose to measure—the readability of headlines by discussing such factors as reader familiarity and text visibility. Of greatest relevance to more recent work—though less ambitious than that which computational approaches now permit—is her comparison between her own sample and a broader sample of text types, which includes informal speech, fiction, serious talk and writing, and scientific writing.

Turning to studies of the language of advertising itself, we see that there are occasional examinations of the topic in more general works on genre analysis. Among scholarly examples of this type of treatment is Bhatia (1993), and a useful pedagogical review of the subject can be found in O'Donnell & Todd (1991). Still of great value, however, is Leech's (1966) much-quoted study, which surveys the types of linguistic devices used by British writers and designers of display advertising. Like Straumann (1935) in relation to the language of headlines, Leech is primarily concerned with analyzing the specialized grammar of advertising. He notes the disjunctive nature of much of this language, and he details some of its salient features. Among these are the low frequency of function words such as articles, auxiliaries, and pronouns; a preference for nouns over verbs and adjectives; and heavy nominalization over predicative constructions. Working within a tradition of literary criticism, Leech also describes advertising language as a *subliterary* genre, arguing that, as in literature, the advertisement writer often relies on unexpected strategies of novel and creative exploitation of language within predictable linguistic patterns and techniques. Thus the writer's rhetorical aim—here, attracting and sustaining the reader's attention, making the advertisement memorable, and prompting the reader into appropriate action—is met by systematically setting off a familiar pattern against inventive use. Even today, Leech's study continues to provide a useful catalog of the defining features of this language variety. Despite the fact that they represent the state of the art in Britain some three decades ago, his taxonomies also continue to provide useful distinctions, although, as Coleman (1983) points out, they may or may not correspond to what viewers actually perceive. The principal relevance of Leech's study to the present analysis of CAR, however, is that it is one of the first attempts to explicitly link in a full-length study the functional parameters of the advertising genre with its linguistic manifestations, or in other words, to apply the notion of systematic register variation to the language of advertising.

In a more recent and broader survey of British advertising in the printed press, billboards, and television, Guy Cook (1992) expands the narrow linguistic formulations of the discourse of advertising in general. His aim is to show that texts construct meaning through interaction with other types of discourse. He examines the interface of linguistic form with visual, musical, and paralinguistic features. He considers pragmatic issues such as shared knowledge and stance in an attempt to explain more precisely how readers of advertisements come to understand these texts. But the most original aspect of Cook's work is his analysis in Bakhtinian terms of the social implications of advertising language. Drawing on illustrations from a variety of advertisements, he shows how texts can create, evoke, and reinforce dominant social types, especially sexual ones; and he argues that a sense of self as both an individual and a participant in social activities is to be found within the form of discourse, not outside it and independently from it, in the language of advertising as in all language use.

In a much shorter study, Toolan (1988) follows Leech (1966) in concentrating on the stylistics of conventionalized and formulaic aspects of the language of advertising in the British press. Like Leech, Toolan sets out to uncover the recurrent structural patterns of the variety, without which, he argues, advertising language would not be recognizable as a distinct variety. Borrowing once again from a tradition of literary analysis, he shows how patterns are set up, then exploited and creatively departed from against a background of formulaic repetition. He describes some of the functional parameters of the genre but stops short of relating them quantitatively to their linguistic manifestations. However, he provides what could serve as a generic description of the study of register variation in general when he writes that advertising language is

> always underlyingly functional, but usually far from mechanical. There are many different types of format and content as there are different types of product, and the problem for the advert[isement] writer is always one of appropriacy and effectiveness, on the basis of how the product is viewed, how the target audience is viewed, and given the constraints of the newspaper or magazine context. (p. 53)

In addition, Toolan warns against the small, highly selective, and possibly subjective corpora that often form the basis of studies of language variation. An analysis of the language of advertising, he argues, should not be based on a single type of ad since this might lead to premature, unrepresentative, and possibly tendentious conclusions. Instead, a corpus should as much as possible reflect diversity of style and strategies, even if this approach leads to the destruction of possibly fictitious notions of unified genres.

In a more extensive study, Geis (1982) concentrates on the linguistic devices favored by producers of television commercials. Much as Leech (1966) had done for the British printed press, Geis reviews some of the linguistic features that recur in the language of TV advertising in the United States. This includes a detailed study of comparatives, similes, noun compounds, and count versus mass nouns. However, Geis addresses not only how advertisers use language but also how consumers are expected to interpret it. While this allows him to claim that his focus is essentially psycholinguistic in character, his study could be more appropriately described as pragmatic since what he offers is primarily a theory of communication rather than actual psycholinguistic experiments that might test the comprehension of TV commercials. More specifically, Geis's approach to relating the encoder's intention and the decoder's perception is essentially Gricean (Grice, 1975)—that is, comprehension depends less on the decoding of the meaning encoded in symbols than on the inference of meanings and contextual information not explicitly carried by these symbols, guided by a mutually agreed upon set of interactional rules, or *maxims*. He proposes a scale of relative strength for these maxims (expanded to six from the original set of four). He goes on to argue that the maxim of relevance—the assumption on the decoder's part that all elements in a message must be relevant to the current interaction, however linguistically incoherent they may appear—is paramount in the process of recovering meaning.

Like Geis (1982) and Guy Cook (1992), Coleman (1983) goes beyond a description of the language of advertising itself; she sets out to address psycholinguistic aspects of the interaction between the encoder and the decoder in an attempt to explain how consumers of advertising come to understand what they do. What makes her study especially noteworthy is her examination of the role played by phonology and prosody in conveying the advertiser's intentions.

But like Geis, she mostly addresses issues of comprehension from a pragmatic angle. In particular, she argues that viewers need to make two distinct but complementary types of inference. One type of inference—which might have been termed *linguistic*—is based on the audience's knowledge of the structure and conventions of the advertising genre. This includes not only nonstandard syntax and the ubiquitous recourse to puns that marks much of modern advertising but also prototypical behaviors by the actors represented or referred to in the commercials: announcers, sponsors, supporting celebrities, and so on. The second type of inference—which might be described as *pragmatic*—requires a willingness to abide by a Gricean *cooperative principle* (Grice, 1975) in assuming, for example, that content will be favorable to the product.[1]

Like Geis (1982) and Coleman (1983), Tanaka (1994) also proposes to explain how consumers come to understand advertising messages. Using as her data a selection of display advertisements from the British and Japanese press, she argues against purely semiotic accounts of communication, which regard the polysemous nature of linguistic and nonlinguistic messages as a misfortune and an obstacle to communication. Instead she notes that the normal process of utterance interpretation involves potentially problematic reference assignment, disambiguation, and enrichment. She finds fault with both Geis and Coleman, however, for not going beyond the accepted view that the interpretation of advertisements takes more than just decoding and that the audience needs to make appropriate contextual connections. The question, Tanaka argues, is not whether but how preexisting bodies of knowledge play a role in determining the way in which advertisements are understood—in brief, how decoders recognize encoders' intentions. To answer this question, she appeals to *relevance theory* (Sperber & Wilson, 1986), which proposes a maxim of relevance as the single principle of real importance in disambiguating messages. While Tanaka's fervent exposition of relevance theory as the key to understanding the pragmatics of advertising language may strike the theory's many critics as oversimplistic,[2] her study makes an undeniable contribution to a much-needed description of the linguistics and stylistics of the advertising genre.

For their part, Vestergaard & Schrøder (1985) bring an explicit ideological agenda to their analysis of the language of advertising.

In this, their work comes close to analyses of the language of journalism by exponents of *critical linguistics* such as van Dijk (1988) or Fowler (1991). Vestergaard & Schrøder also build on the groundwork laid by Williamson (1983) in her discussion of the ideologies she sees shaping the language of advertising. Like Geis (1982), Coleman (1983), and Tanaka (1994), they aim to go well beyond a formal description of the medium. But they stay largely clear of pragmatic considerations and set out instead to expose "the individualized collective deceit of advertising" (p. 174) and to reveal "the really insidious ideological processes which treat a phenomenon as so self-evident and natural as to exempt it completely from critical inspection and to render it inevitable" (p. 145). Thus while advertising can be an agent of change—at least to the extent that changing fashion constitutes change—it is also a means to prevent social change or even to assume that change is impossible.

Turning now to the rare studies of classified advertising proper, we see that Ayres (1992) focuses on the relationship between levels of communication apprehension (CA) by writers of personal ads and the presentation of information in their texts. Although his case is seriously weakened by his failure to define CA or to specify how this construct was measured, he notes that writers of personal ads with high CA tend to emphasize personal characteristics (such as height or hair color) and exclusions (such as age limits) regarding potential partners. This is a finding that may be relevant to analysts with an interest in information structure, as I will show in my discussion of information structure in classified ads.

To my knowledge, one of only two studies devoted primarily to the linguistics of classified advertising is Nair (1992). In this short but ambitious study, Nair examines a corpus of personal—or rather, since they are placed by families, not individuals, matrimonial or even matchmaking—ads drawn mostly from the Indian press. She justifies her attempt to combine the study of form with that of ideology in this medium on the grounds that "both overt and covert ideologies associated with particular literary forms and gender, genre, and grammar intersect in especial ways in culturally specific varieties of the 'matrimonial column'" (p. 231). Reflecting an influential strand in the linguistic analysis of the 1990s, Nair notes that "a study of this subvariety of written language is of theoretical interest both because it has considerable human and social implications and because in form and style it is quite amenable to strictly linguistic analysis" (p. 232). She argues further that "it is more important to explore the consequences, presuppositions, and implications of grammatical constructions than simply to postulate skeletal rules of grammar that perfectly describe a discourse" (p. 250). Thus she sets out to uncover the underlying structure of these texts: the linguistic structure via a system of rewrite rules and tree diagrams and the pragmatic and ideological structure through the use of Hallidayan terminology such as the *medium* or *beneficiary* of an utterance.

Finally, my own study of the language of personal ads (Bruthiaux, 1994) contrasts with the pragmatic and ideological concerns of the work reviewed here. Much as Leech (1966) does with display advertising, I present a description of the linguistic form of this medium in an attempt to isolate some of the salient linguistic features of these highly specialized texts. Among the features described and exemplified are the use and distribution of articles, pronouns, auxiliaries, modals, negation, copulas, and prepositions. The study also notes the distinctive syntax of relativization, the high frequency and inventiveness of lexical compounding, a preference for unusually long adjectival and nominal chains, and a overall disregard for the literary grammar. Given the dearth of detailed descriptions of simple registers—and of the register of classified advertising in particular—and given the ever-present danger of premature theorizing before enough linguistic facts have been established, it is this classificatory approach that I propose to follow in much of this book.

Source and nature of the corpus

The corpus on which this study is based consists of 800 ads drawn in equal numbers from two Los Angeles newspapers, the *Recycler* and the *LA Weekly*.[3] A total of 100 ads was selected from each of four categories in each newspaper: secondhand autos, personals, apartments for rent, and job offers. Aimed at an affluent and trend-conscious readership, the *LA Weekly* specializes in entertainment-oriented items but also reports social and political issues of local interest. Drawing on a much more diverse population, the *Recycler* is one of a number of newspapers, now found in many cities worldwide, devoted exclusively to classified advertising. Raising most of its income from its relatively high price on the newsstands, it offers free advertising for most types of ads, with the exception of personal ads, for which a charge is made. Reporting a weekly circulation of 170,000 over the greater Los Angeles area and a readers-per-copy ratio of 2.75, the *LA Weekly* claims to be read overwhelmingly by single people (82%), with nearly half the readership (47%) in the 25–34 age group. Slightly over half the readers (53%) are college graduates. Almost a third of them (28%) have an advanced college degree, and nearly half (45%) are professionals. No comparable demographic data are available for the *Recycler* beyond a claim of a weekly circulation of 40,000 for the central Los Angeles issue, from which half the CAR corpus is drawn.[4] However, a lower socioeconomic status of the readership can be supposed from the fact that the newspaper is essentially a means of locating inexpensive autos, accommodation, and household items. This supposition seems to be supported by a higher than normal readers-per-copy ratio of 3.5.

Randomized sampling was used to neutralize the wide degree of variation in the number of ads printed in individual sections of both newspapers. In particular, the numbers of lines are not directly comparable since the column width varies between the newspapers. Selection criteria, described in full in appendix B, were meant to ensure that the corpus represented the full range of auto makes, apartment locations, job types, and ratio of women seeking men to men seeking women as partners.

Typically, a classified ad runs to about three or four lines, although auto ads tend to be somewhat shorter than the other three categories. Inevitably, however, a number of advertisers try to achieve greater saliency by ignoring spatial constraints and writing very long ads. To determine how this register might be produced under consistent spatial constraints, I decided on an upper limit of six lines. This was based on an (initially) casual observation that very few ads appeared to exceed this norm except those obviously designed to catch the eye, usually by being boxed, preceded by an unusually large heading, or both. Those that exceeded the norm were excluded from the corpus. While the number of deviant ads varied from category to category, a total of 233 (6.6%) of the 3,547 ads available for inclusion in the corpus were rejected on the basis of excessive length (table 2.1). Since it represents well over 90% of the available ads, I take this sample to be a fair representation of CAR at work.

A major characteristic of CAR is the use of abbreviations (see appendix C for a glossary of abbreviations appearing in ads cited throughout this book). As a result, measuring ad length in terms of the number of words means confronting the perennial problem of what to count as one or as two words. Little internal consistency is found in the corpus, even within one section of the same newspaper, especially when it comes to hyphenation. Thus somewhat arbitrary decisions had to be made and applied consistently to ensure that conclusions based on word counts were not distorted by typographical variation. While there are obvious risks involved in this approach, it remains valid provided that it eliminates more anomalies than it creates.

Because pricing policy can affect what is treated as separate words, the same lexical item often appeared in several typographical forms in the original. Thus all slashes, hyphens, and periods were removed, and conventionalized sequences such as *full-time*, *n/smoking*, or *t.o.p.* were counted as one word, as were standard abbreviations such as *SWF* or *DJM*. Conversely, category-specific sequences such as *in/out*, *grey/black*, or *emotionally/financially* were divided into their component words. All telephone numbers were counted as one word,

Table 2.1 Percentage of available ads excluded from the corpus due to excessive length (over 6 lines) (total ads available: 3,547)[a]

Ad category	% of ads excluded
Autos	6.3
Apartments	6.8
Jobs	7.1
Personals	6.1
Recycler	6.4
LA Weekly	6.9
All ads	6.6

[a]*Recycler*, Nov. 7, 1991. *LA Weekly*, Nov. 29, 1991, and Jan. 10, Jan. 31, 1992.

with all punctuation and spaces removed, regardless of original appearance. Finally, it was decided that to record accurately and consistently the frequency and distribution of all function words in the corpus, contractions should be restored to their full form before the word count was performed. Thus apostrophes were treated as spaces in short forms of verbs, auxiliaries, and negatives. For example, items such as *I'm, let's, you're, who's, what's, that's, can't, doesn't, won't,* and *don't* were treated as sequences of two free morphemes and counted as two words.[5]

The word count, which totals 16,075 words as just defined, reveals a degree of variation in length in the texts represented in the corpus. Whereas the cost of an auto, apartment, or job ad is linked to the number of words, personal ads can be placed up to a maximum number of words for a set fee, the price rising sharply for each additional word. This explains the lower variation in ad length in this ad category (personal ads: 2.4 standard deviations measured in the number of words per ad; other categories: 5.1 to 5.3 standard deviations) (table 2.2). As noted, mean length varies little in apartment ads (20.9), job ads (20.0), and personal ads (21.6), although it does in auto ads (17.9 words per ad). This may represent a convention or perhaps the smaller range of statements that can be made about an auto as opposed to an apartment and, especially, a job or a potential partner. Finally, no obvious variation is noted between the two newspapers. Thus the sample appears to be representative of the register as a whole in text length.

Table 2.2 Mean ad length as measured by number of words (N = 16,075)

Ad category	Mean	SD	Low	High
Autos (n = 200)	17.9	5.3	9	37
Apartments (n = 200)	20.9	5.1	10	40
Jobs (n = 200)	20.0	5.3	8	34
Personals (n = 200)	21.6	2.4	15	31
Recycler (n = 400)	20.1	5.3	9	40
LA Weekly (n = 400)	20.1	4.5	8	37
All ads (N = 800)	20.1	4.9	8	40

The CAR genre needs little introduction for autos, apartments, and jobs. Typically, ad writers show a preference for a stark, to-the-point style. There is predictable variation in lexical choices across ad categories. Auto ads mention tires, apartment ads refer to furniture, and job ads highlight salaries. At first glance, there is also a prima facie case of systematic variation in the degree of syntactic elaboration as measured by the ratio of function (grammatical) to content (lexical) words, and the issue of a possible correlation between this variation and the functional parameters that shape these texts will be pursued further. Typically, writers appear to elaborate syntactic structure only minimally, as in the following:[6]

(1) 86 MAZDA 626LX. 87,000 mi. Fully
    loaded. 5 spd. Runs great! Needs
    paint. $3500. Call David (213) 829-1234

(2) BRENTWOOD, lovely lrg 2+2 condo, 2
    parking spaces, sec grg, all built-ins, grt loc,
    w&d, carpets & vertical blinds thru, $1100 mo.
    310-285-1234

(3) FEMALE bodybuilder ndd for sports &
    exercise tv show, must be vy muscular & well
    defined, xlnt pay 310-553-1234

Personal ads, in one form or another, are nothing new. In addition to showing their pervasiveness in the Indian press and their importance in structuring matrimonial relationships in that country, Nair (1992) cites a source that claims that the form was already common in eighteenth-century England, with the earliest record dating back to 1746. Today, personal ads are no longer just a quirky, big-city phenomenon. Instead, they have become a feature of many newspapers and magazines worldwide. In the Los Angeles area alone, personal ads appear on a daily basis in such major publications as the *Los Angeles Times* (in English) and *La Opinión* (in Spanish). Numerous other newspapers of more local interest and countless ethnic publications also feature these ads on a regular basis. Internationally, the spread and popularity of personal ads can be gauged from the columns of the *Recycler* itself, which in a typical week may print as many as 2,000 of these ads. Electronically linked to over 75 similar publications in 25 countries, the newspaper reflects the growing worldwide appeal of the variety, with Brazil, Britain, and, increasingly, eastern Europe strongly represented.[7]

According to Nair (1992), personal (or in the case of Indian newspapers, matrimonial) ads show "distinctive features of lexis, syntax, and discourse organization which set it starkly in contrast with other classified advertisement" (p. 232). Immediately characteristic of many English language personal ads is a reliance on descriptive three-letter abbreviations. Thus readers need to know (or quickly learn) that *SBF* stands for *single black female* or *DJF* for *divorced Jewish female*. Some writers make highly imaginative use of literary techniques such as alliteration and assonance. Others resort to the highly conventionalized choice of an opening word beginning with the letter *A* since this usually guarantees publication toward the top of the section. A typical personal ad might be the following:

(4) ARTISTIC, HEALTHMINDED, AU-
BURN haired beauty with brains
and bod, seeks SWM 30–40 with
depth, looks, success and sincerity
under his belt. Call #1234

Occasionally, wordings appear to suggest expectations by the writer of immigration rather than matrimony. Personal ads are also a frequent source of amusement for casual readers, and they could easily be dismissed for having only peripheral information to offer on language use. Yet they are the expression of genuine personal circumstances, which motivate language users in broadly similar fashion, a feature that makes these texts especially amenable to the study of language variation.

Representativeness of the corpus

While educated guesses can be made about the social identity of some of the language users in the corpus, I am not concerned here with a possible link between social dialect and register. The fact that certain linguistic features serve to mark both dialect and functionally conditioned language is widely accepted. In addition, according to Finegan & Biber (1994), membership of a particular social group is taken to correlate with manifest competence in the range of registers born of the near-identical situations in which members of that social group are by definition regularly involved. Indeed, shared familiarity with these situations and with the registers that go with them is a major factor in identifying these individuals as members of a specific group. This is not to deny that there may be substantial socioeconomic differences between the two readerships. After all, I am proposing to compare the *LA Weekly*, a publication once described as "hipper-than-thou" (*The Economist*, November 14, 1992, p. 25) with the *Recycler*, an unglamorous collection of mostly free ads for mostly secondhand items. Yet the competence demonstrated by all CAR users in handling this register suggests that, for this purpose at least, they should be regarded as a homogeneous group. Thus despite the risk that some of these variables may not be entirely factored out by the exigencies of identical language purpose, uniform spatial constraints, and powerful stylistic conventions, I need not be further sidetracked by issues of socioeconomic status, age, or native-speaker competence.

A more central question arises concerning the size of the present corpus, which with 16,075 words drawn from two newspapers may appear insufficiently representative of wider classified ad practice in English. Certainly, further work in this area should aim to survey a larger corpus drawn from a wider range of publications. But in focusing initially on this corpus, I assume that a randomly selected specimen (one publication or two) of the species (newspapers) is no less likely to represent the wider species than a much larger sample. Comparable studies of specialized registers often appear to rely on relatively small, sometimes quite narrowly based sources. It is true that Leech's (1966) study of the language of British advertising covers a relatively broad corpus of 617 TV commercials and his commentary includes illustrations from some 190 separate sources. But Janda's (1985) study of the simple register of academic note-taking (NT) is based on a corpus consisting of sets of notes taken by seven different persons listening to one lecture each. Ferguson's (1983) analysis of sports announcer talk (SAT) examines 13 segments of unspecified lengths that total 10 hours and are drawn from American recordings of baseball and football commentaries, with additional data from Japanese and other conversational sources. Romaine's (1994) study of SAT in Tok Pisin is based on an unspecified number of issues of one newspaper published in three separate years, and it gives no indication of the overall size of the corpus. For none of the above corpora are actual word counts given. Thus while no direct comparison between these and the present analysis of CAR is possible, the present corpus appears to be of a size broadly in keeping with recent research practice.

Also potentially troublesome is the variation in editorial practice across publications aimed at different readerships. An examination of three other local newspapers with substantial sections devoted to classified ads (the *Los Angeles Times*, the *Orange County Register*, and the *Los Angeles Reader*) suggests that limited variation does exist but that it appears to be editorially imposed (as in the greater or lesser use of abbreviations or in patterns of information sequencing) or imitatively transmitted (as in greater or lesser lexical creativity). The claim for the homogeneous nature of the CAR corpus also needs to guard against the possibility that some ads may be composed collaboratively over the telephone, typically those for autos, apartments, and jobs, as personal ads may only be placed by mailing a set form. Although the practice was likely to have affected both newspapers equally, an informal check was made of the extent to which any part of the CAR corpus may have been subjected to editorial interference. This was done by placing four ads in the *Recycler* under four related headings (see appendix D for details of procedures together with texts as dictated and printed). If a degree of standardization were editorially imposed, this should show up across the four headings as alterations to the original scripted text. In the event, texts were printed precisely as dictated, with no alterations to information sequencing and only some abbreviations edited in. In brief, it is not likely that either set of editorial conventions would be so different and processes of standardization so powerful that they would play a part in shaping CAR texts. Thus, despite the limitations I have outlined, the present corpus appears to be broadly representative of CAR, and it is to the task of describing this register that I now turn.

3

Syntactic elaboration

The job of comparing one language variety with another normally presupposes the identification and operationalization of linguistic variables, be they lexical, morphological, or syntactic. This is normally done by identifying a set of linguistic features that can be expected to appear in specific slots—or obligatory contexts—in the literary grammar and by measuring their actual occurrence in the variety under examination. These actually occurring features are then quantified as a proportion of possible occurrences, thus permitting the computation of what might be called structural reduction in this variety.

A common problem with a quantitative approach of this type is that language users cannot always be relied upon to produce enough examples (henceforth, *tokens*) of a given feature, especially once a decision has been made—as is the case here—to observe only natural language, generated outside any experimental context.[1] A second, more register-specific reason for being wary of a purely quantitative approach is that, as I have already mentioned, one of the major characteristics of this register appears to be the relative rarity of precisely the kind of syntactic features—such as articles, auxiliaries, or pronouns—that lend themselves readily to comparison and quantification and whose presence is taken for granted in more syntactically elaborated language. As I will show, the level of syntactic elaboration in many CAR texts is so minimal that the very concept of syntactic structure—and with it the notion of obligatory context—becomes largely irrelevant. Identifying which features may be missing from which structural context is thus so dangerously judgmental that the validity of data extracted on this basis must be questioned.

In partial response to these methodological problems, I concentrate here on what is essentially a description of what makes this register distinctive. My starting point is an assumption that the stringent spatial constraints under which CAR texts are composed are likely to rule out items such as function words that are normally required by the literary grammar but whose presence may be viewed by both writers and readers as nonessential. Following Ferguson (1982), I also assume that at least some of these features will be shared with other simple varieties such as baby talk (BT), foreigner talk (FT), and pidgins, and my description ranges over items listed in Ferguson's typology of features of simple registers (reproduced in full in appendix A). These include articles, pronouns, auxiliaries, copulas, and prepositions. My description also covers strategies of negation, relativization, coordination, and subordination.

As noted earlier, CAR appears at first glance to be characterized by a low frequency of many of the listed items. To be sure, quantification of these items as a proportion of their possible occurrence in the literary grammar should not be attempted. But this does not preclude quantifying their occurrence in this register as compared with their occurrence in other registers to determine just how low this frequency is in CAR. This can be done simply by comparing counts for specific items in this and other varieties—namely, the frequency of a set of features reported by Ferguson (1982) to be largely absent from simple registers with their frequency in much larger and wider corpora.

For this wider representation I turn to the *LOB* (London-Oslo-Bergen) corpus of British English (Johansson & Hofland, 1989) and the *Brown* corpus (Francis & Kučera, 1982), an American English source.[2] Both corpora survey written data drawn from 15 categories, further broken down into a number of subcategories. The very aggregate nature of these corpora will of course mask a great deal of variation across categories and subcategories, especially since no counts are available for each subcategory—none of which includes language drawn from either display or classified advertising. As a result, it is possible that even the highest count for a given feature in one subcategory of *LOB* and *Brown* may be lower than the lowest count for that feature in a narrow register such as CAR. However, the object of the exercise is precisely to gauge the degree of syntactic elaboration of CAR texts—that is, the extent to which the register resembles or, more probably, differs from, wider language use, without recourse to notions of obligatory context.

Characteristics of syntactic elaboration in classified ads register

Definite articles

Discussions of the English definite article stress its role as a marker of endophoric reference, referring the decoder to information that is given because it appears explicitly in previous discourse or in a subsequent prepositional phrase or relative clause (Hawkins, 1978, 1990). An example from the corpus is the following:[3]

(1) STYLIST WITH CLIENTELE
 wanted at one of <u>the finest salons in West L.A.</u> Call Monday–Friday 10 am–7pm . . .

But conditions of production predict that relatively few tokens of the article will be found in CAR, where constraints on space do not permit much expansion of the discourse and where an entity is not likely to be referred to explicitly under different syntactic or discoursal conditions.

As predicted, the definite article is much less frequent in CAR (1.9 per 1,000 words) than in both *LOB* (68.3 per 1,000 words) and *Brown* (68.1 per 1,000 words). (See table 3.1 for all frequency counts discussed in this chapter, in raw form and normed per 1,000 words.)[4] In other words, the frequency of the definite article in CAR is only about 3% of its level in the combined *LOB* and *Brown* corpora, in which the article is by far the most common single item, occurring very nearly twice as often as the next most common word.

The other major role of the definite article is to establish reference exophorically—that is, independent of any mention of a referent in the text itself (Hawkins, 1978, 1990). In this case, the referent is

Table 3.1 Frequency of selected syntactic features normed per 1,000 words

Corpus	No. of words	Definite articles N	Definite articles Normal	Indefinite articles N	Indefinite articles Normal	Pronouns N	Pronouns Normal	Do auxiliaries N	Do auxiliaries Normal	Modals N	Modals Normal	Negatives N	Negatives Normal
CAR[a]	16,075	30	1.9	70	4.4	135	8.4	6	0.4	92	5.7	95	5.9
LOB[b]	1,000,000	68,326	68.3	25,394	25.4	71,390	71.4	4,117	4.1	13,923	13.9	9,647	9.6
Brown[c]	1,014,000	69,016	68.1	26,651	26.3	71,248	70.3	4,183	4.1	13,870	13.7	9,240	9.1

Be copulas N	Be copulas Normal	Prepositions N	Prepositions Normal	Relative pronouns N	Relative pronouns Normal	Coordinating conjunctions N	Coordinating conjunctions Normal	Subordinating conjunctions N	Subordinating conjunctions Normal
84	5.2	587	36.5	23	1.4	398	24.8	7	0.4
36,418	36.4	87,031	87.0	8,146	8.1	36,450	36.5	2,209	2.2
32,933	32.5	86,995	85.8	7,707	7.6	37,300	36.8	2,197	2.2

[a]Classified ads register.
[b]London-Olso-Bergen (*LOB*) corpus of British English: S. Johansson & K. Hofland, *Frequency analysis of English vocabulary and grammar*, Vols. 1 & 2 (Oxford: Clarendon Press, 1989).
[c]*Brown* corpus of American English: N. W. Francis & H. Kučera, *Frequency analysis of English usage: Lexicon and grammar* (Boston: Houghton Mifflin, 1982).

assumed to be uniquely identifiable from the shared context hinted at by the definite article itself. Since it represents a short cut to referential assignment, this is precisely the type of feature that should be used by writers operating in a spatially constrained register.

It is not surprising, therefore, to find that in the vast majority of cases, definite article use in CAR occurs in unusually elaborated clauses and sentences—mostly in personal ads, in which the referent must be recovered from a culturally common context:

(2) SBM, 30, looking for black or Hispanic
 girl to go with. No drug users. I like
 going to <u>the movies</u> & <u>the beach</u> . . .

In other cases, texts can include an entire segment that has become conventionalized to the point of acquiring idiomatic value and, presumably, of resisting manipulation or reduction:

(3) VIDEO SALES "B" Movie Distribution has inside sales positions for
 people with <u>the gift of the gab</u>. Call
 Michael . . .

But it is the absence of the definite article that gives CAR part of its characteristic appearance. From a perspective that sees grammar as homogeneous and largely independent of functional factors, it should be straightforward enough to identify missing definite articles and, by restoring them to the slot from which they have presumably been deleted, to construct a text that meets the requirements of the literary grammar. However, although an element is often omitted, it is not always clear what it might be since several alternatives are often available. This is true even in relatively richly elaborated texts (typically, personal and job ads), where there is a chance, for example, that the absent segment might equally be a definite article, a possessive pronoun, or a noun:

(4) BORN again Christian, SBF, 33, sks SM
 who loves God, over 5'11", under 40, can
 see beyond outside <u>straight to heart</u> . . .

Despite this lack of a definite article, referential assignment is mostly not problematic since enough contextual clues have normally been offered earlier in the ad to make the article redundant. In the following example, no explicit clues are needed by a cooperative reader scanning a column known to be devoted to apartments for rent to infer a link between *owner* or *manager* and the previous mention of *building*:

(5) NORTH HOLLYWOOD, lrg 2+2, good bldg,
 laundry, dishwasher, pool, gym, play yard,
 much more, <u>owner</u> is <u>resident manager</u>, $800
 mo . . .

In other cases, deictic information is found outside the text, once again making the presence of the article unnecessary:

(6) BEAUTIFUL, PROFESSIONAL
 WOMAN, 31, loving, giving, happy,
 sensual, tired of <u>Big City</u> seeks par-
 adise with beautiful special man,
 best friend lover. Call . . .

In a small number of cases, it is the inherent uniqueness of the head of the noun phrase that allows the elimination of the definite article, with similarly nonproblematic results:

(7) 20, VEGETARIAN, LOVE life, <u>earth</u>
 and <u>sky</u>. Can't believe I'm doing this.
 Long red hair, brown eyes. 5'10".
 Call . . .

 Evidence from the CAR corpus thus confirms predictions that the definite article will not be a prominent feature of this register. Yet its apparent resilience in some strongly idiomatic segments suggests that even the stringent spatial constraints that should impose maximum compression on CAR texts may not be sufficient to overcome the power of conventionalization in this register, an issue I examine further in chapter 4. Furthermore, some apparent unevenness in definite article use across ad categories suggests that spatial constraints do not have a uniform effect on linguistic form across the four ad categories and that other factors may be influencing the composition of these texts. What these additional factors may be and what role they might play is addressed in chapter 5.

Indefinite articles

The English indefinite article indicates that a description is not intended to be defining and that the encoder does not expect the decoder to recover from the context the further implicit information that would define the referent to the point of uniqueness (Hawkins, 1978, 1990). This is particularly true at the first mention of a referent in a text, before repeated reference has established this information as given and therefore uniquely identifiable from within the text, this uniqueness being typically signaled by the definite article. Given the spatial constraints of CAR, it is unlikely that a single entity will be referred to repeatedly. In addition, most autos, apartments, jobs, and even—at least until closer acquaintance—of individuals as potential partners are in the real world very much nonunique. This predicts that the indefinite article as a marker of the nonuniqueness of nouns should appear at least as frequently in this register as in a corpus representative of the language as a whole. The converse would confirm that the article is a prime candidate for elimination from this spatially constrained register.

In fact, the indefinite article represents a much smaller proportion of word tokens in CAR (4.4 per 1,000 words) than in *LOB* (25.4 per 1,000 words) or *Brown* (26.3 per 1,000 words). This translates to a frequency in CAR of about 16% of its level in the combined *LOB* and *Brown* corpora. This is higher than the frequency of the definite article but still low enough to suggest systematic variation between this register and wider language use.

Those indefinite articles that appear in CAR tend to occur in segments that broadly meet the requirements of the literary grammar. This is true even in cases in which the ad as a whole falls short of this standard, and other function words—here, *do* auxiliary, pronoun, and copula, at least—would have to be inserted elsewhere in the text to make it conform fully to that grammar:

(8) NEED <u>A PART-TIME INCOME?</u>
You must have <u>a typewriter</u> or good
handwriting. Hours and location
flexible. Call NOW for details . . .

Noun phrases with and without indefinite articles can even coexist within a single clause, often for no apparent reason:

(9) SWF, 36, sks SWM, over 36, for friendship & dating. No vices. I'm <u>a business
woman</u> seeking <u>professional man</u>. Photo . . .

This lack of systematicity in indefinite article use becomes more noticeable in longer ads containing a higher number of noun phrases:

(10) MANAGER trainee, must have <u>4 yr degree</u> &
some gd sales bckgrnd, must want a
<u>long-term career</u> in <u>growing company</u> w xlnt
benefits & salary advancement potential,
$2000 mo . . .

As in the case of the definite article, however, it is the absence of indefinite articles that makes CAR distinctive. Although in the preceding examples indefinite articles could be said to be unambiguously missing from the slots allocated to them by the literary grammar, the matter is not always so clear-cut. In some cases, a noun may equally be interpreted as count or noncount, thus making insertion of an indefinite article optional:

(11) 82 FORD T-BIRD, V8, auto rust clr pnt, brn,
<u>cloth int</u>, fully loaded, runs & looks grt, $1500—
call . . .

Moreover, in minimally elaborated texts—typically auto ads, consisting as they do of little more than word lists—boundaries between noun phrases can be very fuzzy. As a result, it is not always clear whether a particular noun operates as the head of an autonomous noun phrase or whether it would form part of a previous noun phrase and therefore require no indefinite article of its own:

(12) 87 BUICK ELECTRA. <u>Station Wagon</u>. 46,000 mi. Mint condition. $7500 . . .

In other cases, an item may be treated as a noun phrase in its own right, thus inviting an indefinite article if the text were to be syntactically elaborated further. Or it may be seen as the adjectival component of an implied noun phrase:

(13) 86 BUICK SKYLARK, 1 owner, auto, 46M, <u>4 cyl</u>, cass radio, new front tires, $6000 . . .

In some texts, it can be difficult to tell whether it is an indefinite article or a possessive pronoun that is implied:

(14) ASIAN lady, 36, wants a baby, sks tall hard working husband. N/d, n/s, no drink, please. <u>Letter and photo</u> . . .

More often—especially in auto and apartment ads—nouns occur as part of long lists from which the normal markings of syntactic elaboration are absent. Here insertion of indefinite articles beyond the first noun in a more elaborated version of the text is entirely optional, with stylistic rather than semantic consequences:

(15) 87 MERCURY SABLE LS wgn, auto, V6, fully loaded, tint, <u>alarm</u>, <u>pullout ster</u>, <u>digital dash</u>, <u>snrf</u>, alum rims, 37M, runs xlnt, salvage title, $5500 firm or trd for ? — call pager . . .

Still, it remains true that unambiguous cases of missing indefinite articles are very common in CAR. Virtually all openings of auto and personal ads could be said to lack an indefinite article, clearly reflecting an editorial convention:

(16) <u>PRETTY, FEMININE, ASIAN student</u>, 21. 5'5". 155 lbs. struggling, seeks fantasy fulfillment from tall, kind, attractive, generous executive type. Call . . .

This also affects job and apartment ads, although here a greater degree of creativity in the wording of openings makes the phenomenon less salient:

(17) <u>EXPERIENCED, INDEPENDENT LA ad rep</u> needed at Genre—"Gay version of Esquire." Commissions and bonuses to $20,000 first year! . . .

In all four ad categories it is within the body of the texts that unambiguous cases of missing indefinite articles are most common:

(18) HOLLYWOOD HILLS <u>Spacious 2BR/2BA condo</u>, <u>refrigerator</u>, <u>micro</u>, European cabinetry, <u>pool/spa/gym</u>. Access controlled, gated parking $1200 month . . .

All ad categories—but especially apartment ads—also have tokens of noun phrases consisting only of a compound adjectival modifier with no explicit head noun and no indefinite article:

(19) HOLLYWOOD HILLS $650/<u>1 bedroom</u>, $850/<u>2 bedroom</u>, large closets, views, wet bar and gated parking . . .

In summary, predictions of a widespread role for indefinite articles in CAR are not confirmed by the data. Instead, the indefinite article behaves much like its definite counterpart in being typically left out of this simple register. In this, CAR can be said to resemble closely other simple registers such as BT, FT, pidgins, and headlinese. In addition, I have highlighted some of the difficulties involved in determining the extent to which indefinite articles might form part of syntactically more elaborated, underlying versions of CAR texts before the kind of wholesale deletion that might have given these texts their present form.

Pronouns

Dispensing with pronouns is said by Ferguson (1982) to be a widespread strategy for achieving linguistic simplicity. It is a feature of the interlanguages of second language users regardless of their first language background (Meisel, 1983b). Young children appear to have no serious difficulty making sense of the role assigned to pronouns in the adult input (Chiat, 1986). Yet this ability is not matched by these learners' readiness to use pronouns in their own production, and pronoun use in English generally requires a degree of social pressure if the acquisition and generation of traditionally correct forms is to be achieved by young learners (Cruttenden, 1977).

Generally speaking, the key factors in determining the selection and insertion of pronouns are the pragmatic requirements of the discourse (Mühlhaüsler & Harré, 1990). In CAR, the simplicity of the interaction between a writer and a reader and the generally nonproblematic identification of a referent and an addressee tend to make the explicit insertion of first and second person pronouns largely superfluous. This, as much as the influence of spatial constraints, probably explains why many of the rules that control pronoun use in the literary grammar appear to have been ignored.

Not surprisingly, both personal and possessive pronouns represent a far smaller proportion of all word tokens in CAR (8.4 per 1,000 words) than in *LOB* (71.4 per 1,000 words) and *Brown* (70.3 per 1,000 words). Whereas the frequency of these pronouns in CAR reaches twice that of indefinite articles and four times that of definite articles, it still amounts to only about 11% of its level in the combined *LOB* and *Brown* corpora.

In CAR, both first and second person pronouns occur overwhelmingly in subject position. Many of the first person pronouns that appear in the corpus form part of syntactically elaborated clauses, despite minimal signs of syntactic elaboration in the ad as a whole:

(20) US INTERNATIONAL. <u>We need help in all areas</u>! 50–70K per year for serious individuals. Full-time part-time . . .

Much the same is true of second person pronouns:

(21) ANGEL OR DEVIL? <u>You decide</u>. Nocturnal DWM, 33, seeks pale, petite, gothic SWF, 25–32, sensually flexible adventuress. Are you woman enough? Call . . .

However, a salient feature of CAR is the much larger number of cases in which a personal pronoun is absent from a recognizable subject slot. Although the deixis inherent in the interaction—here writer addressing reader—almost invariably makes referents readily identifiable, elaboration to the standards of the literary grammar becomes dangerously judgmental since a second person pronoun is not the only alternative for the slot. In the presence of uninflected modals at least, a third person pronoun or, with minor adjustments to punctuation and capitalization, a relative pronoun are just as likely:

(22) SALES REP WANTED. <u>Must know LA</u>, Harley Davidson market. <u>Will be selling art</u> limited edition Harley canvases. $500–$5000. 25% sales commission. Sales material will follow . . .

In some cases, a verb phrase with no subject pronoun is placed so close to a foregrounded noun phrase that elaboration to a relative clause headed by a subject relative pronoun is plausible:

(23) ACCOUNTANT, <u>must have 4 yr degree</u> & minimum 6 mo general accounting bckgrnd,

dynamic growing wholesale distributor
company w xlnt benefit pckg, $1900 mo . . .

In other cases, the greater length and complexity of the subject noun phrase makes it harder to choose between a relative clause and a new clause headed by a first person subject pronoun:

(24) SEEKS American Indian! Long-haired
artist/musician +. Attractive SF, 35,
<u>loves your culture</u>. N/s, n/d. Phone/photo . . .

In all of these cases, the availability of two or more possible expansions makes elaboration to the standards of the literary grammar highly problematic. To be sure, this does not constitute evidence that ad writers are not guided by elaborated underlying representation before to the possible deletion of redundant items. What this shows is simply that a single underlying representation cannot be unambiguously retrieved from these texts. In itself, this is a substantial departure from the widespread assumptions of deletion that I referred to earlier.

In contrast, identifying a missing segment as a first person subject pronoun is often nonproblematic because the semantics of a new clause imply a switch in reference between participants or entities—here from commodity to advertiser:

(25) APARTMENT manager wanted to manage 16
or 25 unit bldg, <u>pref</u> mature couple, free 1+1
rental . . .

Other unambiguous cases are those in which the presence of the word *own* as part of an expanded segment would require the insertion of a possessive pronoun in an expanded version of the text. But even this relatively elaborated wording still leaves open the choice of second or third person pronoun:

(26) MASSEUSES WANTED, females
only! Immediate employment, great

pay. 18+ only. Central Valley location. Incalls. <u>Own transport</u>. Tawny. 11–5pm . . .

Although transparent semantics normally make referential nonproblematic, possessive reference is just as likely to be expressed through an indefinite article as through a more explicit possessive pronoun in more elaborated versions of these texts. This frequent feature of CAR tends to follow predetermined syntactic patterns and to occur in predictable contexts, often at the end of job or personal ads. Yet conventionalization is not so rigid as to rule out all creativity or at least permutations of the most common nouns in the sequence, such as *photo*, *letter*, or *phone*:

(27) HONEST Cajun, SWM, 28, sks SWF, 22–32, for friendship, maybe more. <u>Send photo and phone</u>, please . . .

To sum up, CAR texts routinely require readers to rely on contextual clues rather than on explicit personal pronouns for the successful assignment of personal reference. This is of course a widespread feature of spoken language. But the fact that it surfaces here in a written, carefully planned register confirms the view of Biber (1988), among others, that a spoken or written dichotomy has only limited explanatory power. Instead, this suggests that language users are adept at drawing on a wide range of strategies to meet the demands of each communicative situation. Precisely what relationship may exist between the writers' choice of strategies and the functional parameters of CAR is addressed in chapter 5 of this book.

Do auxiliaries

The *do* auxiliary is a prototypical example of a true function word. That is, it is a semantically empty operator whose role is principally to permit the transformation of statements into negations or the formation of questions (Huddleston, 1984). Another function of the auxiliary is as a vehicle for the stylistically marked foregrounding of adverbials. The auxiliary is also associated with the marking of emphasis and contrast, as well as the expression of affect. This combination of functions predicts that auxiliaries should be rare in a spatially constrained register such as CAR.

As predicted, the *do* auxiliary words reach a frequency of only 0.4 per 1,000 words in CAR, whereas in both *LOB* and *Brown* the frequency is 4.1 per 1,000 words. This amounts to a frequency in CAR of only 10% of the combined *LOB* and *Brown* corpora. All six tokens (three negatives and three interrogatives) of the *do* auxiliary in CAR appear in syntactically elaborated sentences:

(28) <u>DO FEMALE ADVERTISERS only await responses?</u> This fit 'n trim 33 yr. sero-pos Libra man seeks pretty-eyed humble older woman. Call . . .

Conversely, unambiguous omission of the cluster of *do* auxiliary and subject personal pronoun represents predictable borrowings from the grammar of informal, typically spoken registers produced in face-to-face interaction in which explicit mention of addressees is often unnecessary:

(29) <u>NEED MONEY</u>? Receive $500–$1500/week part-time stuffing envelopes for reputable California company. Send LSASE to: . . .

This low frequency of the *do* auxiliary in CAR may reflect less the omission from a spatially constrained register of a redundant, semantically empty element than the overall function of these ads, which is to make unambiguous, typically positive statements, not to raise questions or to focus on negative issues. An alternative explanation is that CAR writers can choose to express negation via more synthetic routes that require no dummy auxiliary, thus leading to more integrated texts. This is a hypothesis I consider further in the discussion of negatives.

Modals

Unlike dummy auxiliaries, modals go beyond the role of grammatical operators in that they serve to differentiate between factual assertions and the speaker's view of these assertions (Huddleston, 1984). As Chafe (1985) notes, predications are normally made and interpreted on the basis of a shared assumption that their content is factual, and it is only in a minority of cases that the question of reliability enters the picture, or at least is linguistically signaled. In addition, many languages rely on verbal inflection or suffixing for the expression of affect. Examples are the subjunctive forms of romance languages or the final particles of many Japanese or Korean honorific forms. In contrast, English typically takes an analytic route, which requires the presence of an independent word. This predicts that a register devoted to the presentation of the principal characteristics of autos, apartments, jobs, and potential partners will make sparing use of modals since spatial constraints should limit writers' ability to hedge their statements and to express their stance toward the propositional value of their utterances, even if they wanted to do so.

As predicted, modals occur at a lower rate in CAR (5.7 per 1,000 words) than in *LOB* (13.9 per 1,000 words) and in *Brown* (13.7 per 1,000 words).[5] However, this still represents a surprisingly high 43% of their frequency in the combined *LOB* and *Brown* corpora.

A few of these modals appear in syntactically elaborated clauses, although their removal would take little away from the overall message:

(30) COMPANION /aide wtd, geriatric care
provider, <u>will provide care</u> for elderly,
disabled, or sick person—call . . .

More common are cases in which building up the text to the requirements of the literary grammar would almost certainly require the insertion of a modal, although the exact choice of modal (*must* or *should*, for example) is a matter for conjecture:

(31) EUROPEAN male a must. <u>Be 30</u>, decent,
tall, big, athletic, educated, for a trim
attractive Jamaican SBF, 32. Must write . . .

Possibilities multiply when the pattern is found with verbs rather than copulas. Here the insertion of a modal is by no means an obligatory choice, although it remains a much more likely one than the apparent imperative of the existing text:

(32) WOMEN NEEDED. Unique
housekeeping service interviewing
attractive, outgoing girls. Great
$$$, <u>work topless or lingerie</u>. Call . . .

Even more frequent are texts in which syntactic elaboration is so minimal that meanings—here an employer's preferences—are framed in little more than list form, and the entire cluster of subject pronoun, possible modal, and copula would have to be inserted in an expanded version of the text:

(33) LOS ANGELES, large 1 bdrm apt, <u>employed</u> &
refs reqd, nr Western & King, no section 8,
$375 mo . . .

In other cases, it is a cluster of modal and copula—such as *would be*—which would have to be added, especially when the semantics of the adjective in the predicate strongly express affect in addition to factual assertion:

(34) PRETTY woman, SBF, tall, slender, sks
financially secure older gentleman, rela-
tionship. <u>Foreigners ok</u>. Let's talk . . .

More ambiguous are cases of minimally elaborated texts in which the semantics of enquiry or suggestion are signaled only by a question mark. Here the number of possible verb phrases—perhaps containing a modal—is so high that no single elaboration stands out as particularly likely:

(35) DWM, 36, w/1 kid, sks to complete
that missing link w/you. Earthy, adven-
turous, intelligent, <u>family life, kids</u>? . . .

It is clear from the corpus, however, that writers are adept at finding ways around spatial constraints and that dispensing with the modals that might appear in an expanded version of a text is only one of a number of options. Most noticeable among more integrated alternatives to a complex verbal form that includes a modal is the ubiquitous and register-marking *seeks*:

(36) AN "ELIZABETH" (20, SAF) <u>seeks</u>
 <u>"Mr. Darcy"</u> (20–30, SM) with a po-
 etic love of life and intelligent wit.
 Call . . .

Another frequent alternative to modals is the use of the adjective *possible* where an elaborated version might prefer a less integrated construction that involves perhaps the modals *may* or *can*:

(37) PALMS /Beverlywood, modern 2+2 apt, air,
 frplc, dshwshr, stv, prkng, quiet bldg, <u>pets</u>
 <u>possible</u>, $925 mo . . .

An equally common strategy consists of relying on the semantics of the term *preferred* in a partially elaborated passive construction. This conveys attitude more economically than the active alternative, which might have to incorporate the modal *would*:

(38) PERSON needed part time to make costume
 jewelry, <u>experienced preferred</u>, must be
 reliable—call Mon–Fri 10am–5pm . . .

Another familiar strategy consists of offering a choice, not explicitly by means of an elaborated verb phrase involving the modals *may* or *can*, but simply by listing and contrasting two alternatives:

(39) SPA attendant wtd for phones, reception rm
 cleaning, able to follow procedures, $6 hr +
 tips & bonuses aft training, <u>day or eves</u> . . .

To conclude, although the spatial constraints of CAR may not favor the relative fragmentation resulting from the inclusion of modals in texts, ad writers are not short of alternative strategies whenever the expression of affect is considered essential. This suggests that despite spatial and other constraints, the communicative purpose in economy registers need not be purely informational but instead may include some of the interpersonal factors not normally associated with the compressed texts of an economy register.

Negatives

Huddleston (1984) argues that negation at its most unmarked should be encoded in a form that makes the contrast with its positive counterpart most salient. English typically does this analytically by adding the negative element *not* to the verb phrase. While this type of negation may appear to the analyst more structurally straightforward than synthetic alternatives such as prefixes, its status as the unmarked form may be based more on transformational tradition than on direct observations of frequency. For example, the analytic negative is widely reported to be rare among users of nascent pidgins and late-acquired among both first and second language learners, who typically prefer to express negation by placing the synthetic negative *no* to the immediate left of the constituent to be negated, be it a verb or a noun (Ferguson, 1975). In addition, the *auxiliary + not* form can lead to an increase in textual fragmentation and a decrease in informational density (Biber, 1988). This makes it an unlikely candidate for inclusion in a spatially constrained register such as CAR.

Negatives occur at a frequency of 5.9 per 1,000 words in CAR, 9.6 per 1,000 words in *LOB*, and 9.1 per 1,000 words in *Brown*.[6] This amounts to 63% of its frequency in the combined *LOB* and *Brown* corpora. This relatively high figure is especially surprising given the low frequency of the *do* auxiliary noted in an earlier section.

A closer look at the corpus reveals that, despite the rarity of the *do + not* combination, writers are not short of strategies for including the semantics—if not the conventional syntax—of negation into their texts. Of the 95 tokens of negatives in the CAR corpus, 63 (66%) consist of the item *no*. Another 15 tokens consist of structurally indeterminate abbreviations such as *n/s* and *n/d* (*no/non smoking/smokers, no drugs*), which in effect constitute additional tokens of the *no* form.

A few negatives appear in syntactically elaborated segments that also include the copula or auxiliary. All consist of the analytic form *not*:

(40) I'M NOT DEAD YET —my lovelife is!
DWF, 35. Monty Pythonite seeks
emotionally mature thirtysomething
WM interested in torrid stability. Call . . .

More common are tokens of analytic negatives occurring in partially formed segments, typically without the copula:

(41) DWF, 40, Smoke/drink/love/rock. Not blonde, thin, or rich. I'm warm, earthy, fun. Need younger long hair for fun . . .

In contrast, synthetic negation appears in a variety of contexts but never in elaborated segments, as some element—often a copula—is always left out of the verb phrase. This is especially true of a small number of lexicalized *non-* compounds:

(42) DATA control clerk must type 55 w less than
5 errors in a 5 minute test, non-profit
organization nds sharp person for data entry
& other general office duties, benefits, $1650
mo . . .

Of the many tokens of the negative *no*, all appear in segments with no verb or copula. This sometimes reflects circumstances that are so unexpected that they must be specified in the text itself:

(43) LOS ANGELES, 2+1, lrg lvg rm & dng rm, stv,
no refrig, space for w&d, $750 mo . . .

Most, however, are highly predictable and specific to a particular ad category, whether in full or in abbreviated form:

(44) ZIPPY, BRIGHT, BLONDE beauty,
educated cosmopolitan headturner
wishes for SW attractive male over
40. <u>No smoking</u>. <u>No drugs</u>. Call . . .

Although these data confirm the prediction of an avoidance of the *auxiliary + not* form, there is no sign in CAR of the fronting of the negative said by Ferguson (1975) to be typical of the production of first language learners as well as users of registers such as BT, FT, and pidgins, in which fronting typically produces forms—such as *no want!*—that are ungrammatical in any adult native-speaker register or dialect. In CAR, however, negatives satisfy the requirements of the literary grammar in any number of possible expansions—such as *[there is] no refrigerator* or *[you should use] no drugs*.

Be *Copulas*

In his study of the link between copula use and linguistic simplicity, Ferguson (1971) notes that the primary function of the *be* copula is to mark tense and to distinguish between stative and nonstative predicates. Since both types of information are normally available elsewhere in the text or from the context, it is not surprising to find that copulas occur rarely in pidgins (Mühlhaüsler, 1986; Holm, 1988; Romaine, 1988; Todd, 1990). If copulas fulfill no other, more essential role, they should not occur frequently in a spatially constrained register such as CAR.

As predicted, frequency of the *be* copula in this register is low, with only 5.2 copulas per 1,000 words, whereas there are 36.4 per 1,000 words in *LOB* and 32.5 per 1,000 words in *Brown*. This translates to a frequency in CAR of only about 15% of its level in the other corpora combined.

Tokens of the *be* copula in CAR occur overwhelmingly in syntactically elaborated segments:

(45) LOS ANGELES, 2+1, new carpet, new paint,
lrg kitchen, w&d, <u>others are avail</u>, on N Reno
St, N of Beverly, $600 mo . . .

In many minimally elaborated texts, however, it is not clear that it is a copula that should occur in an expanded version of the text because the existing segment could easily be interpreted as a verb in the past simple tense—active or passive—or as a past participle functioning adjectivally:

(46) 85 PONTIAC FIREBIRD, silver, V6, low miles,
air, ps, pb, auto, am-fm, new tires, <u>serviced</u>,
clean, $3900 . . .

In only one case does a *be* copula occur without a subject pronoun:

(47) YOUNGER MAN SEEKS 40+,
pretty, athletic woman. <u>Am</u> 31, tall,
fit, attractive, bright, sensual, creative. Humor, honesty, communication skill a must. Call . . .

This suggests that, to the extent that it occurs in CAR, the combination of copula and subject pronoun forms a strong cluster in which both elements will tend to covary.

One consequence of the absence of *be* copulas is of course the lack of tense marking, which in many cases is remedied by the presence of a present participle. This is most common in predictable wordings such as *seeking* (19 tokens) and *looking* (15 tokens):

(48) CREATIVE energetic <u>rock band, looking</u> for
female dancers for future live shows and video,
no immediate dollars—call Jonathan or Dee
after 4pm . . .

This is also true in less predictable cases in which the insertion of a tense-carrying *be* copula is made redundant by the unambiguous information provided elsewhere in the context:

(49) <u>HIRING THIS WEEK, only</u>. Black
Oriental, Creole and white girls for
massage. Petite and beautiful only
24 hrs . . .

Still, a substantial number of ads leave the assignment of tense and aspect entirely to extratextual clues. In the following example, this requires informed, cooperative readers to infer that the terms *garaged* and *pampered* are meant to cover past care at least as much as present state:

(50) 89 CHEVROLET CELEBRITY Station Wagon. Air. Stereo/tape, cruise control, new tires. Like new condition—<u>garaged, very pampered</u>. Must See! $6395. John . . .

The *be* copula is also frequently omitted before an adjective, which results in an absence of inflection for person, number, or tense. But this is compensated for by the implicit clues given by the referential switch, here from *pets* to the apartment itself:

(51) MID-WILSHIRE, LARGE singles $475 with big separate kitchens. Breathtaking views. Gym, BBQ, sundeck. Low move-in. Small <u>pets</u> ok. <u>Big enough to share</u>. Great for students. Call . . .

This is also true of past participles operating in an adjectival role, often consisting of highly predictable items such as *required* or *wanted*. In these cases, the presence of a subject makes referential assignment nonproblematic:

(52) <u>OUTSIDE salesperson wanted</u> for established & new magazine route, must have dependable car + good math skills, guaranteed salary . . .

Be copulas are also often absent before predicates consisting of a noun phrase, in contexts ranging from the fairly creative to the highly predictable:

(53) SBF, self-supportive, 36, dark complexion, sks SBM/SJM for friendship. <u>No beauty</u>, 180, but lots of fun! . . .

Often, insertion of a copula would be a likely, though not obligatory, wording in a syntactically elaborated version of the ad:

(54) HOLLYWOOD. We make deals. <u>Beautiful new building</u>. Central air/heat. Fireplace. Jacuzzi, gated parking. Friendly manager. 1000 N. Gardner. Wilshire Realty . . .

Yet given that the phrase *Me Tarzan, you Jane* may be said, by reference to FT and pidgins, to symbolize economy registers (see, for example, Bruthiaux, 1994), it is perhaps surprising that the naming of a referent with a noun or pronoun followed by a list of its properties is so rare in CAR:

(55) SWEET & sincere, intelligent lady wanted for fun, romantic times together. <u>Me</u>: SWM, 30, 5'11", attractive, <u>you</u>: SWF . . .

The absence of the *be* copula, typically accompanied by other signs of minimal syntactic elaboration, also marks prepositional phrases, but temporal reference is easily assigned because of the presence of an adverbial:

(56) 90 CHEVY Blazer 4x4, absolutely like new, midnight black. 5 spd, only 15k miles, <u>never off road</u>, all options —$15,000 . . .

To conclude, the *be* copula is a highly dispensable item in CAR, yet there is a sense that the minimal syntactic elaboration of most verbal groups makes any attempt to produce more elaborated versions of CAR texts a largely futile exercise. This has implications for theories of linguistic simplicity, which I discuss in the final chapter of this book.

Prepositions

Huddleston (1984) distinguishes between two broad types of prepositions in terms of their independent contribution to meaning. In one group, there is little syntactic dependence between the preposition and the preceding verb phrase. That is, there is a great deal of paradigmatic variation among the prepositions that can reasonably head a subsequent prepositional phrase (e.g., *before*, *despite*, and *through*). Here, the choice of preposition is conditioned by the semantic content of the utterance as a whole. A second group, which consists mostly of a small set of very short items with relatively little independent meaning (*by*, *of*, *to*, *with*, etc.), is often dependent on the collocational demands of the preceding verb phrase. For example, the presence of the item *of* would be determined by the previous choice of the verb *consist*, while that of *in* would result from an earlier selection of the verb *result*. In practice, many prepositions can operate in either set of conditions, and a full account of preposition use in English would probably view the system as being distributed along a continuum of greater or lesser independence from the verb rather than in terms of a strict categorical distinction. Prepositions can have a variety of functions such as complement, adjunct, or modifier. But like prototypical function words, they do not allow inflectional variation. In addition, they can be said to constitute a closed class despite the presence in the system of complex prepositions such as *aside from* or *by virtue of*, a subgroup that does allow for additions and creativity. Like modals, prepositions as a class are thus prototypical cases of items that fall roughly midway between the closed choices that form the paradigms of *grammar* (including function words) and the open-ended choices of *lexis* (represented by content words) that may enter into an almost infinite number of combinations (Halliday, 1991).

However, the absence of a principled methodology for placing prepositions along a continuum of semantic weight makes identifying their role in CAR problematic. The approach followed here is to select prepositions with an arbitrary 10 or more tokens in the entire corpus. This gives a set of seven items, all falling squarely within a closed class: *for* (217), *with* (145), *in* (91), *of* (69), *at* (31), *from* (19), and *by* (15). In CAR, this set of seven prepositions occurs at a frequency of 36.5 per 1,000 words; in *LOB* the frequency is 87.0 per 1,000 words and 85.8 per 1,000 words in *Brown*. This corresponds to a frequency of about 43% of its level in *LOB* and *Brown* combined.

In all four ad categories, prepositions occur in largely elaborated phrases despite minimal elaboration elsewhere in the ad, including potential prepositional phrases:

(57) 88 DODGE DAYTONA. Black <u>with</u>
Grey interior. PS. P/B. Automatic,
am/fm. Stereo Cass. 28,000 mi, excellent condition. Extremely Reliable. $5000. obo . . .

Very often, however, many of these segments are not sufficiently elaborated to allow unambiguous identification of a missing preposition, even if the segments could be firmly identified as prepositional phrases. In some texts, the semantics of purpose make the preposition *for* a likely candidate for insertion:

(58) LEGAL driver wtd, undercover exp helpful,
<u>tailing & all hours driving</u>, overnight in hotels,
expenses pd, camper xlnt . . .

One possible expansion of these segments might lead to the creation of relative clauses of the *who can* or *who is interested/seeking* types. Equally, the insertion of the preposition *with* is only one of the alternatives available for the expansion of auto or apartment ads since a relative clause (*which includes*) or a participial (*including*) are also possible:

(59) BEVERLY HILLS, bright 1 bdrm apt,
overlooking tree tops, <u>vaulted ceiling, stv,</u>
<u>refrig, dishwasher, air</u>, close to school &
transp, prkng incl, no pets, $850 mo . . .

Syntactic Elaboration

Evidence of missing prepositions also comes from ads in which a preposition is included in an identical context:

(60) SAN GABRIEL, 1 bdrm, $25 credit check, $75 sec, $675 move in spcl, $550 mo—<u>call Irene at 818-575-1234</u> . . .

(61) HACIENDA HEIGHTS, professional decorator 3+2½ exec townhome, spacious 1800 sq', tennis court & pool, pvt security, for lease, $1250 mo—<u>call Jim 213-392-1234</u>

But even if the preposition *at* were the only alternative for these particular slots, these unambiguous cases are too rare to permit any generalization.

Prepositions can also be unambiguously inserted on the basis of the syntactic or collocational requirements of a preceding noun:

(62) LOS ANGELES, large 2 bdrm apt, quiet working person, carpet, stv, blinds, double patio, parking & security, <u>no user nor seller drugs</u>, $675 mo . . .

A missing preposition can also be identified when it normally forms part of an idiomatic or prepatterned sequence:

(63) 33, GREAT LOOKING SJM brownish blonde hair, blue eyes, <u>excellent shape</u>. Intelligent, secure, romantic. Loves outdoors, theatre, arts, travel, jacuzzis. Call . . .

Much more often, insertion of a preposition in a syntactically elaborated version would stem from the semantic content rather than from the structure of the ad:

(64) APPLICATION taker ndd, for loan company, <u>gd environment</u>, <u>airport area</u>, will pay $35 per application + bonuses . . .

In brief, these observations illustrate the range of semantic roles that prepositions are required to play. While prepositions are the normal vehicle for encoding semantic and discoursal relations, some relations can easily be predicted from the semantics of lexical items in the phrase—bathrooms *in* apartments or autos *with* tires, for example. This makes prepositions easily dispensable in a spatially constrained register such as CAR. In contrast, other relations may require explicit encoding because information about their import may not be available from the context—location or direction, for example. This makes some prepositions more dispensable than others. In addition, it is also possible that nonessential prepositions may be introduced into CAR texts as part of an overall communicative purpose that goes beyond the expression of referential meaning. Perhaps some writers—especially in the job and personal ads—are willing to sacrifice their precious spatial resources and to build up syntactic structure in order to index nonpropositional content such as affect or stance. This crucial part of the message might not be carried by the crudely minimalist structures and wordings found in the less interactive texts of auto and apartment ads, and once again, there appears to be room even in this spatially constrained register for more than purely informational content.

Relativization

Fox & Thompson (1990) show that the grammar of relative clauses in English conversation is shaped by a process of instantaneous decision making about structure that takes into account interactants' attention to information flow. Similarly, Pawley & Syder suggest that human perceptual capacities, or what they call the "one-clause-at-a-time" constraint (1983a, pp. 564–565), make it unlikely that the vernacular and literary varieties of the language would have evolved a single strategy for relativization. They argue that relativization in the vernacular is characterized by clause chaining punctuated by frequent interruptions. They show that vernacular strategies of relativization include the stranding of pronouns in the position that the relativized noun phrase would normally occupy in the literary grammar and relativization of a noun phrase out of a deeply embedded clause. In contrast, the integration of information into a complex unit such as a relative clause requires circumstances of production that only writing under prototypical conditions typically affords, especially in planning time and opportunities for editing. Like most writers, CAR writers normally have ample time to plan their texts. But they are also under more pressure than normal to increase the informational density of their texts, and they cannot afford the increase in function words that relativization might entail. This predicts that relativization in its standard form should not occur widely in this spatially constrained register.

In addition, a theory of accessibility on a hierarchy of relativization proposes that it is easier to relativize subjects than it is to relativize objects, nondirect objects, and possessors, in that order (Comrie, 1989). Languages that permit relativization of an item in the sequence are likely to permit it on all more easily relativized items but not on less easily relativized ones. Assuming that the principle applies in a simple register such as CAR, relativization of subjects should be more frequent than that of direct objects, nondirect objects, or possessors.

As predicted, relative pronoun use is low in CAR, with a frequency of only 1.4 per 1,000 words, as compared with 8.1 per 1,000 words in *LOB* and with 7.6 per 1,000 words in *Brown*. This translates to a frequency of only about 13% of its level in the combined *LOB* and *Brown* corpora. Moreover, 22 of the 23 tokens of relative pronouns relativize a subject, with relativization of a possessive accounting for the remaining token:

(65) DYNAMIC, SUCCESSFUL, PROFESSIONAL 49, 6", athletic, terrific sense of humor, seeks intelligent, slender, refined (but foxy) female, any age, who's [sic] biological clock is still ticking . . .

Users of relative clauses show a preference for the pronoun *who* (20 tokens) over *that* (one token) when relativizing a subject. They also relativize animate subjects in preference to inanimate subjects (*which*: one token), despite the fact that in exactly half the ads in the corpus the informational focus can be assumed to be on inanimate entities, namely, autos and apartments.

Most strikingly, all but one of the 23 relative clauses meet the requirements of the literary grammar in full, despite signs of minimal syntactic elaboration elsewhere in the text:

(66) HEALTHY, HONEST, ACCESSI-
BLE SWM 34, arts, nature, travel,
seeks attractive, successful, SWF
<u>who wants to be worshipped</u>. Call . . .

Even in the single exception, simplification is limited to the omission of an indefinite article in an otherwise fully elaborated clause:

(67) CLASSY, ATTRACTIVE SBF with
old fashioned morals seeks tall
prince, 31–45 of any race <u>who's
ready for sincere relationship</u>. Call . . .

However, the presence of a relative pronoun is not by itself a reliable guide to the full extent of relativization in CAR. Much more frequent are cases of largely elaborated clauses from which the only major omission appears to be the relative pronoun itself. In personal ads—where they are most frequent—these segments can be used to describe either side in the interaction. Most often, they offer information about the writer and are inserted in mid-text:

(68) SWM, 24, long hair, 5'11", 165 lbs, <u>likes
music, beach, movies, sports sks</u> SF for
fun & possible relationship . . .

Less frequently, partial relativization encodes information about readers, usually in quite lengthy segments:

(69) WANTED: DWM/SWM, 35–43
5'10"–6'1", dark hair, attractive,
<u>enjoys cooking, laughing, talking,
movies, music, possesses integ-
rity</u>, character. (818) area. Call . . .

The low frequency of partially or fully elaborated relative clauses in CAR predicts that alternative, more integrated strategies will be found in the corpus. These strategies include prepositional phrases, as well as frequent adjectival and nominal chains. In addition, relativization is suggested in all four ad categories by numerous cases of past participles that operate in adjectival roles in minimally elaborated contexts:

(70) 88 HONDA ACCORD LX1, auto, <u>fully loaded</u>,
xlnt cond, $8900 obo . . .

Similarly, frequent present participles could be interpreted as the semantic core of a relative clause, with the more dispensable cluster of subject pronoun and copula omitted:

(71) NEWLYWEDS WANTED: Couples
<u>marrying</u> or <u>planning marriage</u> in
1992 needed for UCLA project. Participants receive $50. Contact Dr.
Williams . . .

Another alternative to a relatively fragmented and spatially costly relative clause is to rely on an infinitive clause:

(72) NEVER MARRIED SWF, 36, attractive, looking for SWM <u>to move to
Chicago</u> and have family. N.S.
No drugs. Catholic. Call . . .

Evidently, CAR writers are not short of integrated alternatives to elaborated—and costly—relative clauses. But on the occasions when a decision is made to relativize in the standard manner, the decision appears to commit writers to meeting the requirements of the literary grammar in full. This suggests that Pawley & Syder's (1983a) and Fox & Thompson's (1990) characterizations of conventional relative clauses as belonging in the literary grammar are correct. To the extent that they are used at all in this spatially constrained register, relative clauses demand elaboration because they constitute a brief and uncharacteristic digression into a somewhat literary, typically written register in which reduction is normally dispreferred or simply unnecessary.

Lexical compounds

English is perhaps uncommonly generous in providing productive rules for the creation of nouns and adjectives through a combination of inflection and hyphenation. However, as Ferguson (1982) shows, a characteristic of simple registers is a preference for monomorphemic vocabulary that is generic rather than specific. There is no reason why the spatial constraints of CAR should limit writers to the unelaborated, largely uninflected core vocabulary that appears to meet the needs of users of other simple registers, especially those of the handicap type. On the contrary, since the aim here is essentially to combine economy with maximum communicative effect, it is likely that writers will make use of the combinatorial possibilities of the language and that the incidence of compounds will be high.

At first glance, compounding appears to be distributed fairly evenly across all four ad categories. However, a number of problems are involved in identifying the degree of compounding in this register, not least because hyphenation is never a reliable guide. Generally speaking, the point at which usage has turned a novel creation into something resembling a single lexical item cannot be determined, and in this corpus many familiar items are spelled as two words:

(73) 86 JEEP CJ-7 <u>Great looking</u> Jeep.
        Must see—Call Kelly . . .

Variation is apparent even in cases of more established compounds, such as *good looking*, . . . *minded*, or *am fm*. One explanation is that this tendency to avoid hyphenation may reflect editorial policy and the need to maximize revenue for the newspaper rather than the writer's choice. Yet internal inconsistency is by no means unusual:

(74) 85 CADILLAC CIMARON. Original
        owner. Automatic, <u>p/s</u>, <u>pw</u>, <u>p.seat</u>.

4 dr, a/c, 56,000mi. Good condition.
$3900, obo. Call Brian . . .

The inclusion of compounds in ads can at times be highly creative, and few compounds appear with any regularity. Even a familiar pattern such as . . . *minded* occurs only three times as *marriage minded* and three more as *open minded* but only once in each of the following forms: *culturally minded, business minded, health minded*, and *like minded*.

Not surprisingly, specific ad categories produce predictable tokens, such as *move-in* (11 tokens) and *built-in/s* (eight tokens) in apartment ads or the item *part-time* in job ads. But originality is especially visible in personal ads, in which only three out of a total of 27 compounds appear more than once: *long-haired, long-term*, and *sero-pos*. Among the many familiar compounds occurring only once are *well-endowed, down to earth, big busted, french windows*, and *hirise*. Also occurring only once are adjectives and adjectival compounds that are less strongly lexicalized and more amenable to manipulation: *long-legged, American-Japanese, high income*, and *left of center*. Among truly creative compounds are the following: *park-like, family free, Monty Pythonite, moonscapes*, and *homebody*.

Creative compounding often co-occurs in all ad categories with minimal syntactic elaboration in the ad as a whole:

(75) 89 CADILLAC FLEETWOOD
BROUGHAM. 21,000 miles, clean,
no dents scratches, warranty to
9/94. Rolls Grill <u>look-a-like</u>. Security
system. $16,775 . . .

To conclude, compounding helps to integrate large amounts of information within narrow spatial constraints. Its frequency in CAR constitutes an example of the implementation of productive linguistic rules in response to circumstances of production and reception. But in CAR this linguistically sophisticated strategy interacts with a tendency to keep syntactic elaboration reminiscent of the more basic strategies favored by users of simple registers such as BT and pidgins. How both processes might operate simultaneously is an issue to which I will return when I outline a multifunctional model of linguistic simplification.

Coordination

Descriptions that take written, largely formal language to be the model from which rules are to be extracted assume that coordination is signaled by conjunctions. This view excludes paratactic sequences such as *I came, I saw, I conquered*, which Huddleston (1984), for example, relegates to the periphery of syntax. In contrast, reliance on mere listing—with the perception of coherence dependent on implicit, extratextual factors—is a major feature of CAR. Thus exclusive dependence on a quantitative analysis of markers of coordination would only partially account for the chaining of propositions in this register. In addition, not all instances of *and*, for example, constitute true coordination since the item often serves as a filler or weak connective, typically in speech (Chafe, 1982; Schiffrin, 1987). Even assuming that a spatially constrained register such as CAR will not contain many costly fillers, a purely quantitative approach would still depend on coordinators being unambiguously identifiable, an assumption that, as I will show, cannot be sustained.

In Huddleston's (1984) analysis of coordination, conjunctions such as *and* and *or* are seen as central to the system because they can theoretically link any number of coordinated items and because their coordinating scope extends over the full range of word classes and syntactic structures. Thus it is not surprising to find that this pair accounts for most of the tokens of coordinating conjunctions, with *and* (327 tokens) and *or* (63 tokens) well ahead of *but* (eight tokens).[7] This set of three conjunctions occurs at the rate of 24.8 per 1,000 words in CAR, 36.5 per 1,000 words in *LOB*, and 36.8 per 1,000 words in *Brown*. This amounts to 68% of its frequency in the combined *LOB* and *Brown* corpora.

Additive coordination

LEXICAL COORDINATION

Even a cursory glance at the corpus suggests that most coordination in CAR is lexical rather than clausal. However, identifying cases of

Syntactic Elaboration

coordination is more problematic than at first appears. With some familiar patterns there is no room for uncertainty:

(76) 88 MAZDA MX6, <u>red & gray</u>, 5 spd, air, am-fm
    cassette, 40M, excellent, $7500 . . .

But given the spatial constraints of the register, it is not surprising to find alternatives to the conjunction *and* for the expression of additive coordination. This is especially common in the minimally elaborated auto ads:

(77) 89 TOYOTA CELICA ST coupe, <u>grey/black</u>,
    auto, power sunroof, stereo cassette, 20M,
    alarm, like new, $9000 obo . . .

As a result, it is not always clear when an expanded version of the text would include a conjunction. But matters are complicated further by the fact that variation in strategies of coordination affects many frequently used pairs such as the *stove/refrigerator* sequence in apartment ads (27 tokens, plus eight tokens of the *s&r* abbreviation), which appears in no fewer than five different configurations:

(78) HOLLYWOOD HILLS 1 BR/BA, liv-
    ing/dining room, cozy courtyard set-
    ting, private, quiet, beautiful garden.
    Includes parking, <u>stove/refrigerator</u>.
    $625 month. Call owner at . . .

Most frequent among these is a slash (12 tokens), followed by a punctuation mark such as a comma (nine tokens), an ampersand (five tokens), and a space (one token). However, the corpus has no tokens of the full coordinator *and* in this context.

Deciding what should count as subordination is equally problematic in the case of the pairs of adjectives that occur frequently enough to become something of a cliché in a particular ad category:

(79) HARD WORKING ambitious, pretty DWF,
    32, <u>emotionally/financially secure</u>, sks
    S/DWM, w/great personality. Attractive . . .

In some cases, coordination consists not of the ad hoc conjoining of semantically independent items but of familiar collocations and largely lexicalized sequences:

(80) OBERON & Naomi are seeking fabulous,
glamorous, bizarre, extraordinary, artists for
<u>up & coming</u> club, any talent or tricks
welcome, you get xlnt film & industry
exposure . . .

Such is the degree of recycling of familiar collocations in specific ad categories that one element in a collocation can often be predicted from the other:

(81) EAGLE ROCK, York Blvd, street parkg, cozy 1
bdrm duplex, <u>water & gas</u> incl, credit check,
$435 mo + sec . . .

This is true whether coordination is marked by a recognizable conjunction or by one of a number of typographical variants:

(82) HOUSECLEANER wtd for Wed or Thurs,
Glendale, must have <u>exp, refs</u> & speak
English, paid by the hour—call aft 6pm . . .

This is not to say that creativity is altogether absent. Some writers are willing to invest some of their precious spatial resources in alliterative collocations:

(83) NOVELIST. NEAL CASSIDY type.
5'10", slim, 37 seeks slender wildcat
between 21–40 for <u>prowling and
howling</u>. Call . . .

Also common and mostly restricted to personal ads are pairs of coordinated adjectives:

(84) VERY <u>CUTE AND CREATIVE</u>
SWM, 36, seeks woman any race or
age who wants a second relationship. Call . . .

More frequent still are unpredictable collocations of lexical items in which the conjunction introduces the last element in a string of nouns:

(85) BRILLIANT, SENSITIVE HUNK.
Have <u>hair, teeth and good job</u>.
Seeking similarly endowed SF, NS,
professional 25–35. Call . . .

CLAUSAL COORDINATION

Although far less common than lexical coordination, clausal coordination explicitly marked by a conjunction does play a part in linking verb phrases in CAR. This affects both finite and nonfinite clauses:

(86) SWM, 31, 136 sks assertive Sf, 19–39,
<u>to play with & cuddle</u>. Martial artists,
cops, & body builders please apply . . .

In some cases, this co-occurs with only partial syntactic elaboration in one of the pair of verb phrases:

(87) <u>TRUE BLUE, UNIQUE and has a</u>
<u>charm about her</u>! Into states of ec-
stasy (which may include you!).
Seeking class, purist (30's–50's) brilliant. Call . . .

Predictably, however, users of this spatially constrained register make frequent use of a number of alternatives to the expression of additive coordination that involves the conjunction *and*. Most common is the omission of the conjunction from its canonical position at the end of a chain. This affects both nominal and adjectival chains, which often consist of more elements than would be considered acceptable in most other registers:

(88) AFRICAN male, 36, 5'11", 190, sks lady
 any race for serious relationship. I like
 <u>cooking, sports, reading</u>. Letter/photo . . .

Much more rarely, the phenomenon also affects verbs, once again creating chains of a length unlikely to occur in any other register:

(89) BILINGUAL RE intern position, <u>learn RE
 bus, track comml properties, prepare reports,</u>
 Mac data entry, work, p.t., min 20 hrs week,
 training, type 30 wpm, RE interest pref—call
 Michael x 2019 . . .

Contrastive coordination

The rarity of the conjunction *but* in the corpus should not mask the fact that contrast need not be marked explicitly. A few writers elaborate to the point of including the conjunction in their texts despite elaborating syntactic structure only minimally:

(90) 87 FORD Escort Pony, blk, 2 dr,
 37k miles, a/c, am/fm cass deck,
 <u>great car, but must sell</u> $5500 . . .

A frequent alternative is for the more integrated adverb *only* (36 tokens) to modify one element in a contrasted pair, leading to greater integration overall:

(91) <u>PETITIONS CIRCULATORS. Registered voters only</u>. Pam . . .

Since users of this spatially constrained register have an incentive to avoid redundant, spatially costly items, it is not surprising to find many more cases in which the semantics of contrast is left to mere apposition:

(92) 84 DODGE COLT, <u>gd cond, nds carb & clutch cable</u>, $500 obo—call aft 6pm . . .

To conclude, CAR writers take advantage of the fact that coordination need not be marked explicitly. In addition, a substantial proportion of tokens of explicit coordination can be linked to largely predictable collocations. Like all registers, CAR is affected by conventionalization. The extent to which this phenomenon may explain the presence in ads—despite spatial constraints—of dispensable items such as coordinating conjunctions is an issue that I discuss at greater length in chapter 4.

Subordination

Subordination is one of the strategies said by Ferguson (1982) to be infrequent in simple registers. Indeed, subordination is so commonly associated with syntactic complexity that reducing the frequency of subordinate clauses is a standard procedure in the simplification of texts as part of an attempt to help second language learners (Cervantes & Gainer, 1992; Leow, 1993) or older persons with reading comprehension difficulties (Kemper et al., 1993).

In CAR both the frequency and variety of conjunction types are extremely low, probably because of a tendency by writers to avoid the spatially costly fragmentation that normally results from the inclusion of subordinate clauses. Even conjunctions as commonplace as *that* or *because* never occur in this corpus. This leaves *if* as the only exemplar (seven tokens), occurring at a rate of only 0.4 per 1,000 words in CAR, as opposed to 2.2 per 1,000 words in both *LOB* and *Brown*. This means that the frequency of the conjunction runs at only about 20% of its level in *LOB* and *Brown* combined, although the figure would fall below 0.1% if the conjunction were added to a set including *that* and *because*.

Despite the fact that spatial constraints would seem to encourage their use, *if* subordinate clauses in truncated form occur only twice in the corpus, making generalization risky:

(93) SAM sks fun Filipino/Hispanic, 20–25.
I enjoy sports, weekend getaways, walks
by beach, possible marriage <u>if right</u> . . .

It is more interesting that the balance of these tokens occurs in more syntactically elaborated clauses. This suggests that—as in the case of relativization—subordination constitutes a brief incursion into a discourse style characteristic of formal, typically written registers, which forces writers to meet the requirements of the literary grammar in full:

(94) RESEARCH SUBJECTS needed for UCLA study of psychological factors in bulimia nervosa. <u>If you have recovered or are struggling with this problem</u>, call . . .

A common alternative to subordination is a minimally elaborated chain of descriptive terms that often mixes nouns and adjectives, in which a final question mark implies that a set of conditions is to be met before a subsequent proposition can become valid:

(95) <u>EUROPEAN GENTLEMAN? STABLE? Fit? Serious. Funny? Tall? 30–40</u>? Call this 35 y.o. pretty, slim, SWF homebody with bohemian to traditional interests. Call . . .

Even more minimalist is the mere listing of features, without any semantic or pragmatic links between them or the specification of any action to be taken:

(96) <u>GLENDALE, new pnt, lrg 2 bdrm, den, vy quiet, car port, laundry, no pets, $750 mo—call</u> . . .

The availability of more integrated, less spatially costly alternatives to elaborated subordination also explains the absence from the corpus of the *that* conjunction. The closest the corpus comes to this use is a single case of subordination with the *that* conjunction left out, in an elaborated, largely idiomatic sentence:

(97) 20, VEGETARIAN, LOVE life, earth
and sky. <u>Can't believe I'm doing this</u>.
Long red hair, brown eyes, 5'10".
Call . . .

According to Biber (1988), this type of subordination, with or without *that* deletion, is most likely to co-occur with private verbs—that is, verbs expressing mental processes such as thinking, understanding, or knowing. In this corpus, the few private verbs that do occur, such as *know* (one token), *learn* (two tokens), and *appreciate* (four tokens), are not followed by a subordinated clause but instead appear to imply a noun phrase as the direct object:

(98) 85 NISSAN 300ZX 2+2, loaded, runs grt, xlnt
cond, must see <u>to apprec</u>, $5800 obo . . .

To conclude, in common with other economy registers, CAR tends to avoid elaborated subordination. Yet a common linguistic outcome does not imply common causes. Whereas alternatives to subordination may be explained in other registers by cognitive or developmental factors, the dominant factor in CAR is likely to be simply that the level of syntactic elaboration required by subordination is prohibitively costly in spatial terms.

Adjectival and nominal chains

A salient characteristic of this register is the frequency of long adjectival and nominal chains. While there is nothing in the literary grammar to specify the number of consecutive items that can modify a noun phrase, both the length of these chains and their pervasiveness would stretch the limits of acceptability in any other registers, including formal written ones.

Adjectival chains are found in premodifying position, almost exclusively in personal ads. Although chains of four or five elements are especially common, strings of up to seven or eight modifiers are by no means rare:

(99) BLONDE, BLUE, SEXY, shapely, pretty, petite, witty writer craves creative, handsome, humorous, sensitive, sexy, tall, talkative, thereabouts thirtysomething, great guy. Call . . .

Suggestions of relativization are particularly strong in chains appearing in postmodifying position:

(100) POLYNESIAN guy wanted, tall, strong, nice, 28–34, by very pretty mix Polynesian lady, slim, sweet. Write or call . . .

Very long chains are commonly broken up into both premodifying and postmodifying segments:

(101) ROMANTIC, HUMOROUS, MUSCULAR SWM, 36. Artistic, passionate, tactile, aware. You, sexy, happy, smart, pleasurable lady, 25–40. Nightlife, active days. Call . . .

Chains of nouns or nominalizations are widespread in all four ad categories. As with adjectival chains, these sequences typically contain four or five items, but strings of seven or eight are not uncommon:

(102) SILVERLAKE CHARM. 30's Spanish courtyard setting. 2BR split-level w/spiral, large BR. Walk-in closet separate entry, french windows, hardwood, eating nook, trac lights, deck. No pets. $895 month . . .

The frequency of these chains thus offers further evidence that CAR writers are willing to dispense with many of the tools of syntactic elaboration such as relative pronouns, articles, copulas, and verbal inflection. Instead they tend to favor more integrated strategies such as heavy modification of noun phrases through listing. This reduces the need for the spatially costly function words that greater syntactic elaboration entails.

Economy language and ambiguity

In Gricean theory, successful language use depends on—among other things—the encoder's obligation to be as brief as possible but as explicit as necessary (Grice, 1975). For Finegan (1987), all language use falls between two ideals: an unwieldy one-to-one correspondence between form and meaning and an unfathomable single-symbol system to cover all possible meanings. These competing mandates interact with a variety of functional characteristics so that the resulting level of linguistic elaboration matches the demands of the communicative situation. In CAR, as in all language use, this interplay between clarity and convenience determines the degree to which compression will be tolerated and the level of explicitness that will be needed.

Given the spatial constraints that shape this register, writers have an incentive to make maximum use of what they take to be shared context between themselves and their readers. From a Gricean perspective applied to written texts (Cooper, 1982), the exigencies of communication are such that encoders will cut corners by relying on decoders' willingness and ability to recover meaning even where none is overtly indicated. Just as writers must not overtax their readers' ability to make sense of implicitness, readers must be willing— as indeed they usually are, even when faced with experimental or schizophrenic texts (Roberts & Kreuz, 1993)—to find relevance in superficially incoherent messages.

Nowhere is this more apparent than in the use of abbreviations, which constitute primary markers of this register. Randomly selected examples from the corpus include *wpm* (words per minute), *SBF* (single black female), and *RE* (real estate). In personal ads, a space-saving strategy consists of reducing key features of the identity of either party to a three-letter abbreviation. Occasionally, ethnic identity is spelled out along with gender:

(103) PRETTY SBF, 5'3", 140 lbs, warm brown
complexion, seeks <u>Jewish or Italian male</u>
for friendship, possible relationship . . .

Far more often, this information takes the form of a three-letter abbreviation, although both the *Recycler* and the *LA Weekly* leave the interpretation of these codes entirely to their readers. Thus it is only contextual knowledge—here, familiarity with the multiethnic nature of modern Los Angeles—and a willingness to apply this knowledge that can allow cooperative readers to interpret frequent codes such as *SAM* as *single Asian male* or *DHF* as *divorced Hispanic female*.

In contrast, some newspapers may print a mandatory application form that explains the most common of these codes in order to standardize abbreviation practice. But for readers of those newspapers that do not, it is largely confidence in the instinctive application of a cooperative mechanism supplemented with contextual knowledge that can lead the writer to expect *SJM*, for example, to be interpreted as *single Jewish male* and not as the theoretically possible *single Japanese male*:

(104) TALL, DARK, HANDSOME SJM,
26, seeks a romantic, attractive SJF
for a caring relationship. P.O. Box . . .

The expectation of a cooperative principle at work also accounts for the fact that deictic assignment is so often left implicit. This and knowledge of collocational patterns and conventions usually allow the intended referent to be identified without difficulty, despite the fact that the list form favored by so many writers sometimes invites two or more constituents to be treated as equals:

(105) BABYSITTER wtd, occasion overnights &
wknds in my home for short trips, 2 & 4 yr old
children, students, Culver City area . . .

Commonly in personal ads, the lack of referential markers makes it impossible to tell for certain whether a description is meant to refer to the writer, the reader, or both:

(106) SF wanted, 21–29, average, easy going,
marriage minded by SWM 35, 6', 150. Artistic, cln, devoted, financially stable . . .

Less frequently, in cases in which both parties in the interaction are known to play different roles, the context acts as the disambiguator of last resort:

(107) RESEARCHER wanted to do research on
residential burglary statistics, etc. <u>will pay</u>—
write to Fernando Sanchez . . .

Occasionally, writers create ambiguities of the *old men and women* type so beloved of syntacticians yet so easily resolved in context:

(108) FAIRFAX/MID-WILSHIRE $850/up.
Spacious 1BRs. 2BR/2BA
$1100/up. Spa. courtyard, <u>gated
parking & views</u>. 110 S. Sweetzer . . .

While minimal syntactic elaboration rarely creates ambiguities that explicit textual clues or shared knowledge cannot solve, it can sometimes lead to double entendres and to the kind of humorous interpretations that thrive on referential underspecification (Nash, 1985):

(109) JUNIOR drafter wanted, structural, type V &
<u>earthquake experience</u> . . .

Misinterpretation can result from an unfilled argument slot:

(110) FILIPINA lady, petite, 43, romantic,
new to USA, adventurous, desires to
meet a kind, decent, n/s <u>man for sharing</u>.
ORANGE COUNTY . . .

Similarly, the omission of a possessive pronoun can invite an interpretation presumably not intended by the writer:

(111) GOOD looking innocent SWM, 20, 5'8, 155,
brown hair/eyes. New to LA, wants to
meet that special girl, <u>age unimportant</u> . . .

Even in substantially elaborated texts, the mere apposition of noun phrases can lead to unintended interpretations:

(112) CURVACEOUS, CUDDLY, SJF.
5'2", varied interests seeks SJM,
48–58, humorous, sincere, positive
outlook, physically fit, attractive.
<u>Westside for quality relationship</u> . . .

Finally, wordings that depend on shared knowledge of mutual exclusivity can also lead to frivolous interpretations:

(113) JAPANESE, HANDSOME
WESTSIDER, 30, 5'7", 140 lbs,
seeks <u>marriage minded</u>, sincere,
warm <u>women</u> (23–33). Race doesn't
matter . . .

In conclusion, reliance on context is of course not specific to this register or even to economy registers in general, spoken or written. However, compared to registers in which more generous circumstances of production allow for more redundancy, CAR texts often seem to place uncommonly heavy responsibility on readers for disambiguating implicit references and for avoiding referential traps.

Classified ads register and syntactic elaboration

Commentators such as Chafe (1985) have noted the many problems involved in identifying sentences in spoken language. But the problem extends beyond spoken language to written registers such as CAR, despite the fact that the written medium should provide ample opportunities for editing. Analysts of natural language and syntacticians alike are familiar with the fact that it is not easy to tell when parataxis ends and syntax begins. For example, an utterance such as *It ought to work better, shouldn't it?* can be analyzed either as a rule-governed variant of syntax or as parataxis, with *ought* and *shouldn't* conjoined simply because they belong to a common semantic field (Matthews, 1981, p. 38). For the analyst of CAR, problems with the building blocks of syntax often begin even below sentence level. At the lexical level, it can be difficult to determine what constitutes adjectives and nouns, especially in the minimally elaborated auto ads. The abbreviation *dr*, for example, can be taken to be part of an adjectival group when followed by a noun:

(114) 88 FORD ESCORT LX, <u>2 dr HB</u>, auto, ps, pb,
am-fm ster, 56M, maroon, lk new in/out, $4595
obo . . .

Similarly, the pluralization of *drs* seems to identify this segment nonproblematically as a noun:

(115) 86 HONDA ACCORD, <u>4 drs</u>, auto, air, 1 owner,
$5900—call . . .

Yet cases of inflection are rare in CAR. This is especially true in the minimally elaborated auto ads, which have only six tokens of *dr* followed by a noun and just two of *drs*. In the many more cases in which the abbreviation *dr/door* is not followed by a noun (37 tokens), it is not clear whether the segment is used adjectivally or nominally, much less whether it is part of an embryonic relative clause or a prepositional phrase:

(116) 88 ACURA LEGEND, 5 speed, <u>4 dr</u>.
Red ext w/grey leather int. Loaded,
with car phone. Low mileage. Mint
condition. Steal = $12,000 obo . . .

Problems can also occur at the syntactic level, especially as reliance on listing can make it difficult to identify the boundaries of verb phrases. This leads to numerous "floating" noun and adjective phrases (Aarts, 1991, p. 54)—that is, segments whose semantic association with a particular constituent is not marked syntactically:

(117) PRETTY, SPUNKY, DYNAMITE
Hispanic female, <u>26, 5'2", Tequila
shooters, dancing till dawn</u>. Looking

>   for rich, handsome man who can
>   iron . . .

But as soon as a degree of syntactic elaboration is apparent, expansion to the standard of the literary grammar becomes easier and largely consists of filling in missing function words:

(118) SUPERINTENDENT construction coordinator
wtd w at least 5 yrs exp in all fields of
construction . . .

In contrast, the minimal elaboration of many texts make expansion especially problematic, especially when the sequencing of lexical items follows no recognizable rationale, for example, in the insertion of subjective notions (*small pet o.k.*) between factual statements (*1BR . . . parking*):

(119) HOLLYWOOD. PARK-LIKE setting. 1BR. Small pet o.k. Parking. Quiet building. $550/up. Call Claudia . . .

Without substantial rearrangement of the constituents, elaboration to a level satisfying the requirements of the literary grammar would require a large number of separate clauses, increasing fragmentation and therefore cost. This tolerance for what in a more standard text would constitute unjustified and uneconomical sequencing is most noticeable in auto ads. Yet it affects texts in all ad categories, as in the following example:

(120) 86 HONDA CIVIC SA Hatchback. 5 spd. White. Moon-roof. Mint Condition. New Tires. New Brakes. 73,000 miles. Original. Owner. $3900. obo . . .

Nor does the sequencing of lexical items follow syntactically consistent patterns, especially in the long segments, which if syntactically elaborated would require insertion of elements such as the copula (*be*), auxiliary (*have*), modal (*must*), and verb (*do*):

(121) ARE you looking for friendship? Must
be mature, fun, honest, great sense of
humor, nice looking, and like big women . . .

Even the normally more elaborated personal ads often disregard consistency in verbal agreement and often show a tendency to switch between first and third person inflection for no apparent reason:

(122) SWM, 37, lean, handsome, professional
from NYC, $ secure. Camping, compu-
ters. Love kids & animals. Sks marriage . . .

In summary, the frequent juxtaposition of syntactically unrelated lexical items shows that CAR texts rely heavily on listing only sporadically underpinned by syntax. Expansion to a level that satisfies the literary grammar is possible only when some syntactic structure is already visible. The circularity of this process suggests that expansion may consist less of restoring texts to any underlying form that may have applied before deletion than of expanding syntactic elaboration within the limits set by spatial constraints.

Summary

In this chapter, a pattern of differentiation between ad categories has begun to emerge. To be sure, the effect of spatial constraints can be seen in the fact that many of these texts do not conform to the requirements of the literary grammar. Yet differences across ad categories have surfaced with sufficient regularity to suggest systematic variation in the effect of functional circumstances and motivations on the linguistic form of each ad category, and further evidence and explanations for this systematic link between functional parameters and the degree of syntactic elaboration will be offered.

Auto ads are characterized by a generalized lack of recognizable syntactic structure, with fuzzy boundaries between constituent phrases and widespread recourse to listing. Typically, they consist of little more than a series of content words. Subordination is absent and coordination rare, except for the frequent occurrence of a small number of conjunctions in predictable lexical pairs. With only the occasional use of articles, pronouns, and prepositions, and little or no relativization, referential assignment must be made on the basis of contextual clues. This makes any attempt at elaboration to satisfy the requirements of the literary grammar largely futile.

Apartment ads display greater creativity and somewhat greater lexical diversity than auto ads; however, they share with auto ads a largely unelaborated appearance that consists essentially of sequences of nouns with little modification and articles frequently missing in normally obligatory contexts. Although many personal and relative pronouns, as well as prepositions, would have to be inserted if these texts were to be expanded, the lack of a recognizable syntactic structure makes it difficult to choose between several possible elaborations. As in auto ads, referential assignment relies mainly on exophoric clues. Subordination is rare, as is coordination, except for frequent tokens of a limited number of conjunctions in strongly conventionalized lexical pairs.

Job ads are more extensively elaborated than the texts in the previous two groups, with a higher frequency of articles, personal and possessive pronouns, copulas, and prepositions. The transparent semantics of the specialized lexis in these texts makes referential assignment mostly nonproblematic, although there are cases of unintentional double meanings due to underspecification. Here, coordination sometimes extends to pairs of short clauses. There is limited subordination of elaborated clauses, as well as some relativization. Indeed, some texts are sufficiently elaborated to permit greater confidence in making the syntactic or lexical choices that expansion would require.

Personal ads share with job ads a greater frequency of articles, pronouns, copulas, and prepositions, often occurring in more extensively elaborated segments. Referential assignment is mostly nonproblematic, but referential underspecification can lead to surface incoherence, almost always disambiguated by the context. Relativization and subordination tend to correlate with greater syntactic elaboration in the clause that they introduce. Personal ads are also marked by the high frequency of a small range of abbreviations and by a high degree of creativity in lexical compounding.

Despite making repeated references to expanded versions of CAR texts, I have avoided committing myself to an assumption that a more elaborated underlying structure forms the basis of these texts before the systematic deletion of dispensable items because, if the hypothesis were plausible, the reduced output could be expected to retain some skeletal outline of that underlying form. In practice, ads show a high frequency of disjointed sequences that CAR, though written, shares with the largely unmonitored form of real-time speech. This indicates that the syntactic consistency characteristic of planned registers, and more generally the requirements of the literary grammar, are of little concern to CAR users. In contrast, I have noted the frequent presence in CAR of a variety of short prefabricated segments, often strongly elaborated internally but syntactically linked to surrounding text only loosely or not at all. To shed some light on this apparent paradox, it is to the role in CAR of these prefabricated segments and of conventionalization in general that I now turn.

4
Conventionalization

I have just shown that a dominant characteristic of CAR texts is their minimal level of syntactic elaboration, a feature that the register shares with other simple varieties such as pidgins, for example. Given that this characteristic is widespread in many simple varieties of language, it is tempting to follow Ferguson (1982) in positing a possibly innate sense in language users of what is dispensable whenever form must be tailored to what spatial, temporal, or cognitive constraints will permit. For their part, sociolinguists and discourse analysts in general tend to assume that form will be responsive to the situational and functional circumstances of each text type. But neither of these two approaches implies that these processes—a possibly innate response and a functional response—apply on each occasion to each slot in the syntactic structure, resulting in novel texts with only minimal, perhaps accidental, resemblance to earlier production. In contrast, the strong sense of déjà vu that permeates language use—and CAR texts specifically—raises the age-old question of whether human beings are "primarily like buses, which travel along regular routes" or "like taxis, which move about freely" (Aitchison, 1987, p. 3). Put somewhat less imaginatively, does most language use consist of familiar segments recycled in more or less predictable sequences in response to recurring demands, or is it the result of a process of assembling smaller components in novel ways on the basis of an abstract system of rules? Most probably, the answer lies in a combination of both strategies. Individuals who set out to compose an ad readily admit to relying for editorial guidance on the newspaper in which their text is to appear. Moreover, given the narrow communicative function of

CAR texts, it is reasonable to assume that conventionalization, prepatterning, repetition, and the insertion of prefabricated segments will play at least some part in their composition.

The notion that conventionalization plays a major role in language use is nothing new.[1] Halliday & Hasan note that "informal narrative and spontaneous conversation are the most open-ended kinds of registers. But we are never selecting with complete freedom from all the resources of our linguistic system. If we were, there would be no communication" (1989, p. 40). Commentators on simple registers (see, for example, Ferguson, 1971; Ferguson & DeBose, 1977; Gibbon, 1985) routinely note the role of cultural transmission and repetition in their operation. Ferguson, for example, writes that "all simplified registers show differences from other registers . . . that are not simplifications" (1982, p. 58). Mühlhaüsler argues that foreigner talk (FT) "tends to be a mixture of cultural conventions and genuine natural intuitions about language simplifications" (1986, p. 106). Nor is it claimed that reliance on previous linguistic environment and purpose affects only simple registers. On the contrary, the insertion at appropriate points in the discourse of ready-made constituents, semiproductive idioms, and other prefabricated modules is seen by Ferguson (1983) as a reliable index of the debt that every language user owes the environment.

Coulmas (1979, 1981), Pawley & Syder (1983b), Tannen (1987), Johnstone (1987), and Levelt (1989) all point out that the recycling of language takes place to a degree that has not been recognized by analysts anchored in a tradition in which the generation of novel utterances is viewed as axiomatic. Based on a tidy distinction between competence and performance, this paradigm does not favor notions of prefabrication, idiomaticity, and recycling of ready-made constituents borrowed from previous use rather than generated by productive rules. In addition, a scholastic tradition of rhetoric that values novelty and originality of expression is not likely to look kindly upon recycled language, especially in written registers. Even when the spread of conventionalized segments is noted, the phenomenon is typically relegated to a minor role in the analysis of language use because of its very automaticity. If what makes human actions distinctive is the fact that they have their source in a "conscious impulse of the will" (Verschueren,

1981, p. 135), it is tempting to regard the manipulation of linguistic structure as a more central exemplar of linguistic production than the insertion of context-specific, prefabricated, and perhaps unanalyzed segments.

Most probably, the pervasiveness of conventionalized, prefabricated segments reflects the nature of a world in which humans are reluctant to admit to too much randomness, a state of affairs regarded as unfortunate by the rational mind and one that may be partially remedied by the recycling of recognizable patterns and collocations, leading in turn to greater cohesion (Norrick, 1987). Ferguson & DeBose (1977), Gibbon (1985), Halliday & Hasan (1989), and Ferguson (1994) all comment that since ready-made segments also act as register markers, they contribute to a sense of rapport through a degree of familiarity. Thus the recycling of familiar items is a strategy through which language users "together create a discourse, a relationship, and a world" (Tannen, 1989, p. 97). But the evolution of standardized strategies in language use must also be linked to the unavoidable recurrence of communicative goals (Coulmas, 1981), especially in narrowly focused registers. As Sinclair writes, "things which occur physically together have a stronger chance of being mentioned together" (1987, p. 320). A crucial consequence is that if commonly used patterns reflect the common concerns and activities of a community, not all the utterances of its members can be given equal status, and it becomes crucial to identify and describe those modules that appear to have special status within the system (Pawley, 1986).

In addition to cognitive considerations, there are powerful sociolinguistic reasons for studying the role of conventionalization in simple registers. Bartsch (1987) suggests that the imposition of conventions and norms—including linguistic ones—is a society's typical response to recurring coordination problems.[2] Since each language user's willingness to abide by the group's norms is signaled by—among other things—recognition and appropriate production of registers (Coulmas, 1979, 1981), conventionalization of language is a reflection of a social system, and its role in the socialization process should not be underestimated. To be sure, conventionalized segments stem directly from the special communicative needs of groups of language users, but they must be used "in accordance with general principles of the development patterns of recurrent messages in the specialized language of particular social groups" (Ferguson, 1983, p. 169).

Conventionalization of language takes many forms, in CAR as in any other register. Some of these forms are quite unambiguous, thus permitting nonproblematic quantification. Among these are abbreviations, for which full forms can readily be restored. Others are less amenable to quantification. Collocations, for example, "range from the well-established and integrated to doubtfully cohesive sequences of words" (Kjellmer, 1991, p. 126). Thus it is not easy—and it may not be desirable—to aim for neat distinctions between what is "freely collocatable, the restrictedly collocatable and the completely frozen" (Coulmas, 1981, p. 6).

In view of these limitations, I adopt an approach to the study of the frequency and distribution of conventionalized sequences in CAR that is both qualitative and quantitative. I consider the possibility that the presence in some texts of dispensable function words may be conditioned by the collocational rigidity of the segments in which they appear. I begin with a description of idiomatic sequences in CAR. This is followed by an analysis of three types of collocations: recognizable sequences of two content words, the recurrence of prepatterned segments in which function words collocate with content words, and the collocation of specific word classes. Finally, I consider the conventionalization of information structure—that is, the degree of predictability in the sequencing of major semantic components in all four ad categories.

Idiomatic sequences

The corpus contains many examples of largely nonproductive segments that have a distinctly familiar ring and appear to have been borrowed from previous discourse. Although they are topic-specific, their use is not limited to CAR. For example, the following text borrows segments from the discourse of a kind of extended TV advertisement—usually known as an *infomercial*—which typically tries to entice late-night viewers to subscribe to schemes designed to help them start their own business:

(1) BE YOUR OWN boss. Answer only
    to yourself. work as an independent
    sales contractor. Earn $5000 monthly.
    No investment required . . .

A few writers of personal ads appeal to shared background by including whole citations in their texts:

(2) COME up & see me some time, if you are
    kind, communicative, committed. I'm
    40+, creative, rubenesque & pretty . . .

Typically, these idiomatic segments are inserted into otherwise weakly elaborated texts, giving the whole the intermittently elaborated appearance that is a trademark of this ad category:

(3) SOMEWHERE OUT THERE is the
    woman for me. Humble, happy, fit,
    honest, sharing, caring, sero-pos. I.
    Libra, 33. You 30–40. Call . . .

Since syntactic elaboration is an inherent part of the idiomaticity of these segments, it is surprising to find them occurring in a register that is supposed to respond to spatial constraints by eliminating redundancy and concentrating on propositional content, thus increasing the ratio of content to function words. However, some variation is noticeable across ad categories as these segments never occur in auto ads, rarely in apartment ads, occasionally in job ads, but overwhelmingly in personal ads. On the surface, this unexpected degree of elaboration appears to be especially costly, given the tightness of spatial constraints. However, the presence in some texts of these idiomatic segments also suggests that, in personal ads at least, building atmosphere and appealing to a shared background play a role at least as important as the transmission of propositional content in conditioning linguistic choices.

Even more characteristically, CAR is replete with abbreviations of various types, a feature that may be said to constitute a defining characteristic of this register. Operating presumably as both short cuts and register markers, these abbreviations occur throughout the corpus and are not likely to be found in any other context or register. This is most noticeable in the majority of auto ads, and to a lesser extent in apartment ads, which often consist of little more than a list of abbreviated content words:

(4) 81 MAZDA GLC, 4 dr, 5 spd, air, am-fm cass, gd int, 105M, $950 obo—call . . .

Three-letter abbreviations that function as identifiers are often found in personal ads:

(5) ADVENTUROUS, INDEPENDENT
SWF, 22. seeks professional, well-educated, caring, secure and adventurous, SM (25–30). Let's make history. Call . . .

Despite the fact that spatial constraints are roughly constant throughout the register, the distribution of these abbreviations varies considerably across ad categories. Based on data from the *Recycler* only,[3] a count shows that abbreviation use is substantially higher in the auto and apartment ad categories, in which as many as 29% of word tokens are abbreviated in some way (table 4.1).[4]

It is important to remember that, as I pointed out in chapter 2 and appendix D, decisions about the presence of abbreviations in a text are not within the power of the writer but are imposed editorially. Yet the result of this editorial policy appears to be acceptable

Table 4.1 Abbreviations as percentage of word tokens[a]

Ad category	No. of words	No. of abbreviations	% of total words
Autos	1,672	456	27.3
Apartments	2,137	625	29.2
Jobs	2,077	343	16.5
Personals	2,147	219	10.2

[a]Data from the *Recycler* (N = 8,033 words).

to ad readers, and the question remains as to why abbreviations should apparently be more acceptable in auto and apartment ads than in job and personal ads.

Part of the explanation lies in the variation in the range of information covered by each of the four ad categories represented in the corpus. Normally, informational range is reflected in lexical diversity within each text type. That is, the greater the variety of topics to be addressed by a text type, the greater the number of different content words to be found in its component texts, each word category (or *type*) being represented by fewer examples (or *tokens*) of that type. Thus the calculation of type-to-token ratios provides a useful way of measuring this informational range. However, as Biber (1988) shows, it is important that these ratios are calculated on the basis of roughly equal sections of text since longer texts might contain a high number of tokens of relatively few types simply because a single topic is referred to more often. Here, the nearly equal size of all four ad categories ensures that ratios are not unduly distorted in this way. In addition, since the aim is to compare ad categories rather than—more conventionally—individual texts, type-to-token ratios are calculated by dividing the numbers of word types by the numbers of word tokens for each of the four ad categories from each of the two newspapers.[5]

Ratios for auto and apartment ads cluster closely in the 0.30 to 0.31 range: that is, 30 to 31 word types are sufficient to account for all word tokens. At the other end of the continuum, personal ads and, especially, job ads display greater lexical variety (0.37 and 0.45, respectively) (table 4.2).[6] Most probably, lower ratios in auto and apartment ads attest to a relatively narrow range of possible referents, making these readily identifiable despite abbreviations. Conversely, the greater range of possible referents in job and personal ads and the lower probability that the same referent will recur in a text make abbreviations more hermetic. It is interesting that both editors and readers appear to share, without consultation, a sense of the degree of textual elaboration that is appropriate to each situation, namely, a sense of the appropriateness of abbreviations in each ad category. Indeed, I will offer further quantitative evidence of an inverse correlation between the frequency of abbreviations and the degree of syntactic elaboration of CAR texts, and I will consider some

Table 4.2 Type-to-token ratios in the CAR corpus

Ad category	Type	Token	Ratio
Autos	1,117	3,573	0.31
Apartments	1,240	4,185	0.30
Jobs	1,805	4,002	0.45
Personals	1,618	4,315	0.37
All ads	5,780	16,075	0.36

functional correlates of this varying degree of tolerance for the compression presumably encouraged by spatial constraints.

Collocation

Following Kjellmer (1990, 1991), I take collocations to consist of well-formed patterns recurring in identical form. Most frequently, though not necessarily (Sinclair, 1987), the term is linked to two-word combinations of both words and word classes, and I include in this definition not only relatively widely studied two-word sequences but also segments of clause or sentence length, a feature that I have already reviewed.

Lexical collocation

Lexical collocations can be defined as recurring combinations of content words such as nouns, adjectives, verbs, and adverbs, normally containing no prepositions, infinitives, or clauses (Benson, Benson, & Ilson, 1986). Like all registers, CAR relies in part on the recycling of such collocations. As with abbreviations, these collocations come in varying degrees of idiomaticity and in the degree of likelihood that they may appear in other contexts. Certainly, many could not be described as idiomatic since their meaning is minimally metaphorical and largely transparent:

(6) FRONT office medical lt accurate typing, 6
 mo exp & a smile, join friendly general
 practice clinic, no uniforms, promotable,

salary-wise, <u>interesting position</u>, benefits & prkng $1500 mo . . .

Just as striking—though fairly infrequent—are collocations that are familiar but not particularly specific to the topic of each ad category. These are especially rare in auto ads, though slightly more frequent in apartment ads:

(7) SILVER LAKE. LARGE 1BR studio/garden apartment: <u>sparkling clean</u>, private yard. No pets. $655/month . . .

Not surprisingly, given the high level of lexical variety already noted in job and personal ads, it is in these two ad categories that the frequency of these collocations is greatest:

(8) WANTED: 10 PEOPLE to <u>lose weight</u> and <u>earn money</u>. No diet, no pills, <u>no gimmicks</u>! Commissions/bonuses . . .

Since these prefabricated segments consist almost exclusively of content words, they represent an efficient response to spatially constrained circumstances. This is especially true of noun phrases modified by an attributive adjective or by a noun in attributive position, in which each element in the sequence conveys an independent piece of specific, crucial information, as in *walking distance*, for example:

(9) WEST HOLLYWOOD, xtra lrg 1 bdrm apt, lrg kitch & dining area, r&s, c&d, lndry fac, <u>walking distance</u> to everything, $590 mo . . .

More often, however, idiomatic or prefabricated segments—such as the ever-popular *meaningful relationship*—appear to owe their insertion in the text less to the need to specify verifiable circumstances than to a desire to appeal subjectively to shared context:

(10) AFFLUENT, ARTICULATE, academic WM professional (recording business), active, fit, enjoys theater, films, travel. Seeks petite, libidinous, WF (32–40) for <u>meaningful relationship</u>. Call . . .

In addition, cognitive factors such as ease of encoding probably also favor the recycling of previously encountered segments. Yet these functional factors need not be mutually exclusive, and the possibility of interaction among them is an issue that I will take up again when I outline a multifunctional model of linguistic simplicity.

Despite the relatively small size of the corpus, some items recur often enough in nearly identical form to permit limited quantification. Ideally, these numerical data should then be compared to a broader language sample, but a minimum requirement for comparing the frequency of specific collocations in CAR and in a wider corpus is that both corpora should consist of natural language. This rules out specialized compilations of word combinations such as Benson, Benson, & Ilson (1986), which are competence-based rather than corpus-based and give no indication of frequency. Turning therefore to *LOB* (the London-Oslo-Bergen corpus of British English), the sheer size and scope of that corpus predicts that it will include relatively few tokens of a great many collocation types. In a highly specialized corpus, in contrast, it is likely that a small number of categories of specific collocations will occur repeatedly.

This difference should not affect basic categorization, however, and I follow *LOB* in selecting four main word classes for study—namely, nouns, adjectives, verbs, and particles—in order to survey the probabilistic tendencies of some of these combinations and to evaluate the possibility that they may constitute conventionalized sequences. This should permit some comparison of the frequency of specific items between CAR and a larger corpus whenever frequencies are high enough in both corpora to allow meaningful conclusions to be drawn.

Nouns

Given the relatively specific content of personal ads, it is not likely that this ad category will share many of its collocations with a wider corpus. For example, the 17 tokens of the term *life* in CAR represent 16 collocation types, with only the collocation *good life* occurring twice:[7]

(11) ENJOY GOOD LIFE with genuine
nice guy, 31, 6', 175, scientist law
student, historic houses, outdoor adventure, seeks companionship of attractive, intelligent gal. Call . . .

Moreover, the term is found repeatedly in collocations of the *for life* type, as in *for life's joys* or *mate for life*, none of which appears in the *LOB* list of frequent collocations:

(12) LIONESS SEEKS MATE for life!
Call me irresistible, call me adorable,
call me whimsical, but call me . . .

Even more predictably, the term *girl(s)* also appears in personal ads, where it collocates with an attributive adjective in eight out of nine cases. Yet the only collocation to occur more than once is the item *nice girl* (two tokens):

(13) NICE girl, 35, 5'6", 110, sks SWM, 30–43
for long term relationship, enjoy moun-
tains, beach, camping. Photo please . . .

In addition, none of the collocations of the noun *girl* in CAR is listed among the most frequent collocations of the term in *LOB*.

Other examples of collocations that are altogether absent from *LOB* include *flexible days & hours* [three out of 24 tokens of *day(s)*], or—predictably, given that CAR is in effect a Californian corpus whereas *LOB* is a British source—*2-car [parking]* (five out of 23 tokens of *car*):

(14) AUTO restoration for cars from 50's to 60's, need person to help in mechanical, pnt, body & uphols, tops, general detail work, <u>flexible days & hrs</u>, must have experience . . .

(15) HOLLYWOOD. 2BR/2BA APT.
avail. <u>2-car garage</u>, parking spaces,
fplc, balcony, Jacuzzi, sauna. $795.
Call . . .

Even less original are the environments in which the noun *condition* occurs, mostly in auto ads. Of 83 occurrences, well over half (47) are accounted for by the item *excellent*, with *good* (12 tokens) and *mint* (eight tokens) accounting for much of the balance:

(16) 81 BUICK REGAL, full power,
65,000 mi, <u>good condition</u>. $2000 . . .

Proportionately more frequent are nouns such as *home*, which occurs in *at home* in five cases out of 15, and the category-specific *security building*, which accounts for 12 out of 49 tokens of *building*:

(17) HOLLYWOOD AREA, new <u>security building</u> with parking, single, loft available. $500 up. Special rate this week . . .

Given the especially narrow subject matter of auto and apartment ads, choices within a word class are few, and frequent items tend to collocate with word class rather than with word type. Among these is the noun *view*, which collocates with adjectives in 10 out of 18 cases, with only *great* and *fabulous* recurring more than once (two tokens each):

(18) SILVERLAKE. 1920's ART DECO
building in great neighborhood. Everything new. Includes utilities, laundry, security entrance, <u>fabulous views</u>. 1BRS from $525 +. Move-in Bonus! . . .

Greater collocational rigidity is found in a number of register-specific nouns not occurring with sufficient frequency in *LOB* to be included in that corpus. For example, collocations of the term *opportunity* with *special* (two tokens) and *excellent* (two tokens) account for four out of nine tokens, all of them in job ads:

(19) MASSEUSE - SPECIAL OPPORTU-
NITY. Relocate, Peaceful, secure,
world class resort. Legitimate. Furnished, beautiful accommodations,
jacuzzi, pool. 2 openings only . . .

In the same ad category, all tokens of the noun *pay* collocate with adjectives, with *excellent* and *good* accounting for five of the eight tokens, and *money* collocates with verbs in six out of seven cases (*earn*, *make*, *need*: two tokens each):

(20) HANDICAPPED. UNEMPLOYED.
Make money stuffing envelopes.
Send self stamped envelope to Domestic Associates . . .

Many frequent terms tend to occur in a fixed position in a given segment. One example is the term *fun* as a noun, with 11 tokens in the corpus. Of these, all occur in personal ads, with nine in the initial position in a sequence of nouns:

(21) DWM dad, 28, 5'10", 155, brn/grn,
career, sks feminine, caring female, for
fun, quiet times, romance. N/s . . .

Of the 22 tokens of *friendship*, eight occur as the only noun in a prepositional phrase, with one sandwiched between two other nouns. In contrast, 13 tokens occur in the initial position in a segment most often placed toward the end of a text:

(22) ARTISTIC, WARM, HUMANITAR-
IAN, SWM, 44, seeks warm, intelli-

gent lady, smoke and drug free <u>for
friendship, love, family</u>. Call . . .

In many cases this sequencing probably reflects pragmatic or chronological realities, as in *fun, quiet times, romance*. But this clearly does not apply to the term *fun*. Instead, what the frequency of the pattern strongly suggests is a conventionalized and often recycled pattern of alliteration.

Adjectives

A frequent example of a category specific adjectival collocation is the item *new tires*, which accounts for 16 of the 25 tokens of *new* in auto ads:

(23) 81 MERCEDES 280E. Power windows, doors, sunroof.
<u>New tires</u>. Mercedes wheels, a/c.
Looks great. Runs beautifully. Reduced $7700. obo . . .

Here the pairing is simply a means of transmission of, presumably, factual information. Similarly, all four tokens of the adjective *special* in the corpus collocate with nouns or pronouns referring to persons, in contrast to *LOB*, in which all of the many occurrences of the adjective collocate with nouns expressing notions, as in *special case*, for example:

(24) WM, Christian, wants to have fun with a
<u>special gal</u>, movies, outings, talking,
dine/dance, bowling, share-n-care . . .

Another use of the adjective *new* that suggests category-specific conventionalization is *new to*, which is absent from *LOB* but appears in five personal ads, each time in a different context:

(25) PRETTY, fun loving, 25, blond, recently
<u>new to CA</u>, 5'4", 108 lbs, looking for cute,
fun, honest man, who can show me CA . . .

Conventionalization is also visible in sequences that include relatively dispensable terms such as the intensifier *very* in collocation with the adjective *clean*, a combination that accounts for 12 of the 35 tokens of the adjective, all of them in auto ads:

(26) 81 PLYMOUTH CHAMP, vy clean, runs grt,
 must sell, manual trans, $1500 obo . . .

In contrast, none of the nine tokens of *clean* in apartment ads is intensified. Little originality marks the expression of this notion, with only *super*, *extra*, and *sparkling* occurring in the intensifier slot, each with only one token each.

Another common item is the adjective *good*, with 56 tokens distributed across all ad categories, representing a total of 37 different collocations. Other familiar collocations include *good sense of humor* and *good pay*, each with three tokens. Once again the dominance of one collocation (*good condition*: 12 tokens) reveals a lack of lexical creativity characteristic of auto ads:

(27) 87 PONTIAC FIERO, auto, air, new tires, 50M,
 eng & body in good cond, salvage title, $3300 . . .

Even more solid is the collocation *like new*, not found in *LOB* but occurring in CAR on 19 occasions, all of them in auto ads:

(28) 87 CRYSTAL BLUE Yugo GV.
 Excellent cond. Interior/exterior like
 new. 1 owner. Low miles. $1400,
 obo . . .

Finally, the most striking example in the corpus of register-specific conventionalized usage is the adjective *adjacent*, commonly found in *LOB*, and occurring in eight apartment ads:

(29) LOS FELIZ adjac, 1 bdrm, remodeled, large,
 elevator, air, lndry facils, $560 mo: 2 bdrm,
 $850 mo . . .

It is interesting that it is the more integrated [*location*] *adjacent* sequence that dominates (seven tokens), although it would surely be considered ungrammatical in any other register. This repeated wording probably stems from the fact that the placement of location at the head of the ad—to ensure alphabetical listing by area—is itself a conventionalized feature of this ad category. However, for one writer at least, this conventionalized wording is retained despite the fact that it does not occur in the initial position in the text:

(30) SPANISH TOWNHOUSE 2BR/2Ba,
hardwood floors, mini-blinds,
stove/refrig, old world charm. <u>BH</u>
<u>adj</u>. (213) 954-1234.

Thus, whereas while an obligatory pattern of information sequencing generally explains this configuration, the fact that it can occur in contexts in which the constraint does not apply attests to conventionalization at work in CAR.

Verbs

A high frequency of verbs such as *want*, *seek*, *need*, and *call* could be said to constitute defining characteristics of CAR. But while their frequency is high as a proportion of corpus size, their collocational distribution is unpredictable. The more frequent use of the past participle *wanted* (81 tokens, mostly in job ads) suggests conventionalization in that it represents a preference for emphasizing the target of the ad before mentioning the recruiter or duties, a pattern of information sequencing that dominates in this ad category:

(31) MECHANIC <u>wtd for</u> outboard mtr rpr, low hp
Johnson & Evinrude, part time yr round job,
Marina Del Rey, $8.50 per hr . . .

Yet collocational choices for object complements shows little uniformity, with *wanted for* and *wanted to* representing only 17 and

10 tokens, respectively. Moreover, the almost prototypical opening *Wanted:* . . . occurs on only six occasions:

(32) WANTED: HARDWORKING indi-
       viduals to double-check addresses
       by phone for mass mailing. $7/hr. salary.
       Full and part-time available.
       Call Terry at . . .

Most probably, usage of both *required* and, especially, *wanted*—as in the now legendary police posters—may have gradually ceased to be obligatory in the initial position because these words led to loss of saliency in long, alphabetically sequenced columns.

Conventionalization is also seen in the distribution of the frequent term *seek* (143 tokens, almost all in personal ads), which collocates mostly with adjectives. This stems from the dominant pattern of information sequencing in this ad category, in which writers tend to be mentioned before readers:

(33) TALL, attractive rocker SWM, 31, n/s
       intelligent, romantic, adventurous, sks
       similar, liberal SWF for relationship . . .

Although tokens of the term *need* divide more or less evenly into active and passive forms (26 and 32 tokens, respectively, mostly in job ads), the form *needed for* (15 tokens) dominates *needed to* (five tokens), suggesting less conventionalization than the greater integration afforded by the prepositional and nominal alternative over an infinitival construction:

(34) RETAIL SALES clerk needed for
       gourmet store. Must work week-
       ends. Say Cheese . . .

Another predictably frequent verb is *call*, with 146 tokens in 19 different collocations. Of these, 105 tokens (80%) consist of just two predictable types: *call [name]* (63 tokens) and *call [number]* (42 tokens):

(35) HOLLYWOOD. OLD WORLD
charm. Havenhurst Apts. All Utilities
paid. Move-in. Specials w/lease.
$395/up. Singles/Bachelors/1BRs.
<u>Call Anna or Mark</u> (213) 465-1234

Equally solid—though less frequent—is the collocation of *meet* with private verbs, namely, *desire, wait, want, love,* and *wish,* each of which occurs just once:

(36) BEAUTIFUL COSMOPOLITAN
BLACK lady, 25, <u>wishes to meet</u>
conservative professional SWM
over 40 . . .

Finally, the verb *ask* shows how collocations impose on CAR texts some of the features of written texts that are free from spatial constraints. While the corpus has five tokens of *ask for*, it has just one of *ask*, found in a weakly elaborated auto ad:

(37) PONTIAC FIREBIRD '82 very good
condition, fully loaded, black. $3600
or obo. <u>Ask Erik</u> . . .

Given that this unexpected omission of the preposition is admissible to at least one writer, its retention in most cases is further evidence that collocational strength may indeed encourage the retention of dispensable items in CAR.

Particles

The fact that verbal particles are the object of a separate and lengthy section in the *LOB* analysis of collocations reflects their spread across many registers of modern English. In a spatially constrained register, however, phrasal verbs are not particularly efficient since single-word equivalents can provide greater integration. It is not surprising, therefore, to find few tokens of phrasal collocations in the CAR corpus. The only particle to occur with any frequency is *up*, with 11 tokens, most commonly in the category-specific *and/& up* (five tokens):

(38) $595 AND UP. Spacious 1 BD, pool,
jacuzzi, gated parking, close to
downtown, quiet building . . .

Yet not even this collocation makes it into the broadly based *LOB* list of sequences that include a particle.

In summary, although signs of textual integration are common in CAR texts, writers do not always opt for the least spatially costly strategy available to them. This suggests that the insertion of dispensable items in CAR can be traced in part to the very rigidity of many of these conventionalized segments, an issue to which I turn next.

Structural collocation

In contrast to the view of collocations as well-formed, continuous segments, Renouf & Sinclair (1991) propose the notion of *framework* to describe discontinuous strings of two function words with open slots after each one, as in *the* [x] *of* [y]. These are not freestanding, and whether they are well formed, as well as collocationally rigid, depends on what goes into these slots. One salient feature of CAR is that the kinds of function words that form part of these frameworks tend to occur much less in CAR than in a wider sample of language. While tight spatial constraints can be offered as a plausible explanation for the relative scarcity of function words in this register, accounting for their presence in some texts—especially in some ad categories more than in others—will require a demonstration that special functional factors are at play. One possibility is that the retention or omission of function words in CAR may be conditioned in part by the role played in these texts by prepatterning and structural parallelism, and it is to investigate this possibility that I now return to many of the function word types I examined earlier.[8]

Definite articles

If the structural rigidity of prefabricated segments leads to the inclusion of some dispensable elements into CAR texts, this does not appear to affect definite articles substantially since occurrence of the article is extremely low. In contrast, the corpus is rich in segments from which a definite article is unambiguously missing. Yet reference is normally nonproblematic, and in some cases the truncated result has become so conventionalized that insertion of a definite article would seem odd. These cases include the relatively rare item *same* (three tokens):

(39) WANTED: partner/friend, DHF, 38, 6'3",
proportionate, athletic, conservative, pro
n/s, sks S/DWM, 40–45, Same qualities . . .

These also include all 76 tokens of the category-specific acronym *obo* (or best offer), which in substantially expanded form would probably require a definite article:

(40) 85 CHEVY Citation, 4dr, ps.pb,
am/fm, tilt wheel. 49k miles—$1750
obo—123-1234

Also strongly conventionalized are frequent references to location in noun phrases without a definite article. In only one case is the article inserted:

(41) FULL TIME DRIVER with reliable
vehicle wanted for weekday deliveries. Must be pleasant self-starter
with a knowledge of the greater Los
Angeles area. Call Glen . . .

In contrast, no fewer than 31 tokens of the word *area* appear without an article, mostly in apartment ads:

(42) 1BR STARTING $695. Full size
kitchen, a/c, dishwasher, carpet,
pool, laundry. <u>West LA Area</u>. Tel . . .

This pattern also affects less frequent wordings for specifying locations (eight tokens):

(43) ENCHANTING COURTYARD
APARTMENTS <u>in heart of West
Hollywood</u>. Singles. 1 & 2 Bdrms.
Call . . .

Another common context in which collocational force does not lead to inclusion of the article is that of *beach* (seven tokens):

(44) $40,000/YEAR! READ BOOKS and
TV scripts. Fill out simple "like/don't
like" form. EASY! Fun, relaxing at
home, <u>beach</u>, vacations. Guaranteed paycheck. FREE 24-hr. recording . . .

This compares with just two tokens of the same word preceded by the article, both in more extensively elaborated clauses. Other examples are *theater* (two tokens), *arts* (two tokens), and *opera* (one token):

(45) A VERY SMART, 25, seeks SWM.
Erudite on pop culture, literature,
Chinese food, <u>opera</u>? Rather live in
NYC? Call . . .

Thus the aggregate picture is one in which collocational strength does not offer substantial resistance to the compression forced by the spatial constraints of the register. If the insertion of dispensable function words such as definite articles is to be accounted for, other factors—from spatial to interpersonal—will have to be invoked.

Indefinite articles

The presence in CAR of indefinite articles correlates somewhat more closely with the recycling of prefabricated and idiomatic segments. Most probably, removal of the article would cancel out any processing advantages—among others—derived from recycling these familiar segments:

(46) WE GIVE UP! Venice Blvd. street repair is killing us. Rock bottom prices available on 2 & 3BR luxury apartments w/all amenities. <u>Make us an offer</u> . . .

In general, indefinite articles tend to be found in the more elaborated segments of weakly elaborated ads. In some cases, texts include several segments that equally invite insertion of an indefinite article:

(47) LEADING MAN, 30S, hunk <u>with a heart</u>, seeks intimacy and <u>wild passionate sincere relationship with like minded leading lady</u>. Call . . .

Yet the fact that insertion of the indefinite article is evidently not felt to be obligatory in all cases suggests that the collocational rigidity of some segments (here, the item *with a heart*) may be stronger than that of others (here, the segment *with like minded leading lady*). This is especially true of conventionalized expressions such as *a must*, which appears in all ad categories (11 tokens). In some of these segments, the motivation for inserting the article may be to avoid creating a garden path in the direction of a modal:

(48) FINE art publisher nds sales connected agt to dist litho editions immed, <u>enthusiasm a must</u>, gen, commission for results, local or natl, also painting sales . . .

But in most other cases, the lexicalized nature of a prefabricated segment is not enough to guarantee the presence of the article:

(49) REFINED lady enjoys art, music, antiques, outdoors, animals. you: <u>sense of humor</u>, dignified. I'm trim, 50s. Pic . . .

On this evidence, the rigidity of conventionalized segments appears to play a limited role in the occurrence in CAR texts of indefinite articles. Thus it would be rash to see conventionalization as much more than one of the many factors that condition this aspect of the register.

Pronouns

Like indefinite articles, personal pronouns occasionally appear in elaborated, recognizably idiomatic segments, whose purpose may be to hint at a shared culture:

(50) STEP AWAY FROM the norm. You're a SM (21–25), <u>too creative for your own good</u>, seeking creative, idiosyncratic S-mixed-F. (21). Call . . .

A semantic switch—from job to employer or, in the following example, from auto to seller—often makes the identification of the referent obvious, and the rigidity of the segment does not extend to the subject pronoun slot:

(51) 85 TOYOTA COROLLA GTS, 5 spd, air, ps, pb, 2 dr HB, Riken rims, low profile tires, tint, jade grn, 84M, <u>must sell</u>, $3350 obo . . .

Similarly, a nonproblematic switch from one participant to the other explains why object pronouns need not be inserted:

(52) 83 SAAB 900S, 73M, nds trans work, <u>will sell</u> $3000 . . .

For some of these texts, an alternative reading is a relative clause in which the pronoun is raised from object position. Yet the further from the head noun phrase that verbal segment is found, the more likely it is that an expanded version of the text would include a pronoun in object position. This is also true of the frequent cases of *must see* (11 tokens) in auto and apartment ads:

(53) $400 BACHELOR APTS. Mid-Wil-
shire. All new, must see. Skylights.
Art Deco bath, walk-in closets. Great
view in elegantly restored 1920s
building. Call . . .

The frequency of these pronoun-free verbal segments in weakly elaborated texts raises the possibility that they may not in fact consist of verb phrases with missing subject and object pronouns, but of noun phrases with something approaching full lexical value. This notion is supported by the occurrence in the corpus of *must see* in nominalized form:

(54) MID-WILSHIRE, nr La Brea, large single,
sunlight, new carpet, sep eating area, a must
see, $550 mo . . .

Even if this notion must remain hypothetical, it may be worth investigating the possibility that many of these conventionalized segments with missing pronouns may not be the products of the deletion of these pronouns from more elaborated underlying forms. Instead, they may be just as elaborated and complete as the register requires and its spatial constraints permit.

Modals

Given that modals are instrumental in the expression of stance and affect, they should occur only rarely in a spatially constrained register such as CAR. Yet, while I have shown that their frequency was indeed less than in a wider language sample, their relatively frequent occurrence in both personal ads and job ads remains to be explained.

Once again, one possibility is that the collocational rigidity of some segments may preclude the omission of modals even in contexts in which they are relatively dispensable.

The corpus has a few cases of the modals *could* (one token), *would* (one token), and *may* (two tokens), all in elaborated contexts:

(55) HI! sincere SWM, 43, 6' 235, <u>would love
to meet</u> intelligent, slim lady for walks,
talks, hugs or more, must love cats/dogs . . .

Similarly, all nine tokens of *can* (or *can't*) appear in relatively creative and largely elaborated contexts:

(56) 10 SALES people wtd for outside sales job,
$2000–$6000 potential commission a month,
<u>can be full or part time</u>, selling educational
products . . .

This creativity does not apply to the most frequent modals, namely, *will* (19 tokens, including *'ll* and *won't*) and especially *must* (71 tokens, not including 10 tokens of *a must* as noun phrase). Not only are the vast majority of tokens of *will* limited to job ads, but also this modal tends to collocate only with a small number of verbs. This suggests that the modal occurs as part of prefabricated segments peculiarly appropriate to this ad category. Of the 18 tokens of *will*, for example, no fewer than seven collocate with *train*:

(57) GIRLS NEEDED: Attractive Ladies
needed for massage. Professions
W.LA office setting, inexperience
OK. <u>Will Train</u>. Call "California Massage" . . .

Similarly, most tokens of *must* occur in very few collocations, with some two-thirds (46 out of 71) collocating with just four verbs: *sell* (16 tokens), *have* (12 tokens), *see* (11 tokens), and *be* (seven tokens). In addition, while tokens of the modal are found relatively evenly over all four ad categories, each collocation tends to be category-specific. The segments *must see* and *must sell*, for example, are found in auto ads, occasionally in apartment ads, but—predictably—never in job or personal ads:

(58) 84 CHEVY CELEBRITY Eurosport, 2 dr coupe,
air, blaupunkt stereo, auto, loaded, mint, hi
output EFI, <u>must sell</u>, mvg, $2375 obo . . .

Similarly, the segments *must have* and *must be* are largely restricted to job ads:

(59) TELEMARKETING—CALLING
HIGH School coaches. Fundraising
Product. <u>Must have strong work
ethic</u> . . .

However, the strong collocational link tying together modal and verb does not extend to the subject slot.

Negatives

Conventionalization in negation is apparent in the frequency and form of the predictable segment *no/non smoker/smoking*.[9] In only one case (*non-serial killer*) could the negative be said to be used creatively. But in general the distribution of the *no* + *noun* phrase (NP) pattern confirms that ad writers typically call upon a small pool of context-specific, prefabricated segments. In job ads, for example, the phrase *no experience* accounts for seven of the 19 tokens of the negative determiner:

(60) ATTRACTIVE MASSEUSE
WANTED for busy outcall service.
<u>No exp. needed</u> . . .

Similarly, with four tokens each, the phrases *no vices* and *no drugs* account for more than half of all the tokens of the unabbreviated determiner in the personal ads category:

(61) SBF sks SWM, marriage minded, tall,
 40+, I'm 5'9", 185, no dependents,
 <u>no vices</u>, Christian values. Age 40 . . .

In apartment ads, 16 of the 22 tokens of the negative determiner consist of the phrase *no pets*:

(62) SILVERLAKE, 1 bdrm, quiet hilltop, new crpt,
 pnt, mini blinds, appl, pool, laundry, <u>no pets</u>,
 $600 mo . . .

In summary, the use of negative determiners in CAR is accounted for by a relatively small number of predictable types with high frequency and restricted distribution, with just six collocations accounting for over half of the 95 tokens of the *no* + *NP* pattern. While recurrent wordings are probably the products of identical situations, the lack of variation in expressing these notions suggests a degree of standardization from which most writers see no advantage in escaping.

Copulas

As I have noted, copulas are often omitted from predicates that consist of an adjective phrase, especially in predictable contexts. These include the adjectives *necessary* (six tokens), *OK/okay* (18 tokens), and *available* (29 tokens):

(63) $20 an hour cash for glamorous
 beauty to drive private limo for executive. <u>No experience necessary</u>.
 Leave message at . . .

This pattern also applies to a number of predictable past participles operating in an adjectival role such as *required* or *wanted*. For example, none of the 40 tokens of the phrase *loaded* in auto ads is expanded, explained, or elaborated to the point of including the copula:

(64) 82 CHEVY CAMARO Z28, 59M, 4 spd, gd tires,
new pnt, ster, <u>loaded</u>, xlnt, cond, $4200—call
Lori . . .

It is only when the expression occurs in the unfamiliar context of an apartment ad that expansion occurs despite minimal elaboration of the ad as a whole. Yet even here, the copula is not inserted:

(65) BEVERLY HILLS adjc, new bldg, lrg 2+2 &
den, wetbar, central air, video intercom, sec
bldg, 2 car parkg, <u>loaded w amenities</u>, $1650
mo . . .

Most probably, the limited contribution of copulas to explicitness explains why conventionalization of predicates does not extend to this feature. Indeed, insertion of a copula into many of these conventionalized segments would seem quite incongruous.

Prepositions

The influence of conventionalized segments is especially noticeable in prepositional phrases. Most prominent among these is the largely lexicalized item *sense of humor*, which accounts for 11 of the 29 tokens of the preposition *of* in the personal ads category:

(66) SWM, dark hair, grn eyes, 5'11", 163,
needs sexy, patient, SWF, 28–40, loves
cuddling, great <u>sense of humor</u> . . .

In apartment ads, a total of 18 out of 23 tokens of the preposition *of* are accounted for by just two collocations, namely, segments of the *north of* type (11 tokens), and *lots of* (eight tokens):

(67) WESTWOOD, 1 bdrm, woodburning frplc,
patio, blt-ins, 1 blk <u>east of</u> Sepulveda, <u>north of</u>
Ohio, subterranean parking, refrig, stove,
dishwasher, $845 mo . . .

Here, it is the need for explicitness, not conventionalization, that explains the presence of the preposition *of* in this context since the sequence *north of* distinguishes, for example, *north of Hollywood* from *north Hollywood*. But in general, the very rigidity of lexicalized segments such as *sense of humor* or *lots of* accounts for a substantial proportion of the high frequency of prepositions in CAR.

Of course in CAR, conventionalization of what appears to be a prepositional phrase does not guarantee that a preposition (such as *from* or *during*) will always be included in the segment. While types of prepositions missing from their allotted slots are few and highly category-specific, tokens of these are extremely common:

(68) SILVERLAKE AREA. 2BR 2BA, 2
parking spaces, balconies, central
A/C, kitchen appliances, gated
bldg, laundry, cathedral ceiling.
(818) 574-1234 <u>Day</u>. (818) 791-
1234 <u>Night</u>

This pattern is most noticeable in the ritualized openings of virtually all apartment ads, which conventionally begin with location alone since insertion of a preposition would not only be largely redundant but also deprive readers of the convenience of alphabetical sequencing:

(69) <u>MAR VISTA</u>, 2+2, beaut spacious apt, lrg
closets, mini blinds, built-in kitch, big
balcony, sec grg, laundry, nr Sawtelle &
Charnock corner, $900 mo . . .

In this last context especially, the power of conventionalization is such that the lead, containing geographical information without a preposition, seems quite complete, and insertion of a preposition would seem odd indeed, both textually and visually.

Coordination

I have noted the spread of lexical and clausal coordination in CAR. It is not surprising, therefore, to find that the corpus includes a small number of coordinated collocations whose structural strength comes from their frequent occurrence in a wide range of registers and contexts:

(70) FILE clerk /errand, entry, can grow to clerical
/PR & up, must speak, <u>read & write</u> English,
have car in woods, nr beach, p.t. /flexible, day
hrs, TBA, pd miles, $4.25–$6 hr—call Rita . . .

Other coordinated collocations derive their strength from their frequent appearance in a single ad category. Indeed, their repeated appearance in the restricted context of just one ad category makes them prime examples of register markers. In auto ads especially, creativity is often minimal. The phrase *looks and runs like new*, for example, appears in identical form in five ads:

(71) 87 TOYOTA Tercel, 3 dr, 4 spd,
ac, am/fm cass, new batt, fuel
pump, timing belt, <u>looks and runs like
new</u>—$4550 . . .

Permutations are possible, and traces of the pattern are found in *looks & runs great, runs & looks grt, looks great,* and *runs beautifully* (one token each). In addition, some variants such as *runs grt, looks grt* and *runs good, looks good* make use of phonological parallelism, albeit at the expense of word class consistency:

(72) 87 TOYOTA TERCEL, air, auto, <u>runs good</u>,
<u>looks good</u>, $3500 obo—call Miguel . . .

Thus the recycling of conventionalized coordinated segments and minimal syntactic elaboration combine to give CAR much of its distinctiveness, most noticeably in auto ads. But the inescapable conclusion is that, generally speaking, coordinated segments are not sufficiently rigid to explain by themselves the inclusion of function words in some of the more elaborated CAR texts. Other factors that might be invoked to fully account for the presence of dispensable function words in these texts will be the focus of chapter 5.

Conventionalization and discourse structure

So far, I have focused on the conventionalized structure of CAR texts at what might be called the microlevel. That is, I have described some of the recurring collocational patterns affecting quite short strings, from a pair of words to a framework consisting at most of a pair of constituents. I have also analyzed discourse structure at a higher level by considering patterns of coordination between clauses or sentences. But even within a short segment the way in which information is organized depends on organizational patterns in the text as a whole. This is true of the analysis of written discourse of a more conventional type, whether business letters or academic essays. For example, the frequency of passive constructions will depend in part on the degree to which writers wish to stress or downplay interpersonal factors. That is, they may wish to distance themselves more or less from their statements—to maintain the anonymity of a source or to highlight facts rather than the presenters of those facts—all of which must normally follow recognizable patterns for both the propositional and interpersonal contents of messages to be perceived and for their presentation of the whole to be deemed socially acceptable. In conversation also, participants follow time-honored scripts, despite the fact that their largely unplanned exchanges can appear only loosely structured at first. In an opening sequence, for example, a greeting in the form of a question is expected to be met with an answer, not another question. Similarly, a socially acceptable closing sequence requires a final greeting to be preceded by an appropriate chain of preclosing routines.

If CAR is just as bound as any other form of language by the social and other pressures that combine to shape its form, a complete picture of its discourse structure will need to include an account of whatever degree of conventionalization may affect the sequencing of major informational chunks. This is especially true since explicit editorial constraints are weak in this area. Any recurring patterns of information sequencing that may be found in the corpus would be a reflection of a shared sense among writers of what constitutes appropriate discourse in this register, and thus have something to say about the development and maintenance of norms of language in general. However, the radically different content of each ad category predicts that these patterns of information sequencing are likely to be category-specific. Thus, just as it is probably futile to look—regardless of topic, medium, or audience—for consistent patterns of discoursal organization throughout the genres of, say, display advertising or journalism, it is not likely that common discoursal patterns could do justice to both the complexities of a multiparty job search and a simple transaction over a secondhand car. This is why I examine each ad category under separate headings in this section, noting major similarities as and when they occur.[10]

Auto ads

Auto ads invariably begin with an *identifying* segment consisting of year, make, and model, a pattern that is editorially imposed and therefore of little interest to this investigation: *89 SAAB 900 TURBO; 87 MITSUBISHI PRECIS; 88 HONDA PRELUDE.*

Almost equally rigid is the final *transactional* segment, which consists of price and telephone number:

(73) 90 JEEP WRANGLER. 15,000 mi,
 hardtop, 6 cyl. Grey metallic.
 $12,500. (213) 876-1234

In 26 out of a total of 200 auto ads, a contact name is inserted between the two items, occasionally with details of convenient times for calling:

(74) 90 MAZDA PROTEGE, wht, 4 dr, auto, air, am-
 fm stereo, 4 yr extended warranty, xlnt cond,
 must see, $7695—call Richard 213-874-1234

(75) 90 NISSAN 300ZX, 68M, spoiler, chrome rims,
 gold pearl, $17,500—call days at 805-538-1234 or
 eves at 213-255-1234

A limited degree of variation is noticeable in that five ads in all mention no price, and in three others price is separated from contact by additional information. Though small in numbers, these exceptions show that few conventions are so powerful as to rule out variation, provided, of course, that it is editorially or electronically permitted.

Between these two highly conventionalized initial and final segments is usually found any number of *descriptive* segments, which consist of largely verifiable statements: *am-fm cassette*, *new tires*, *anti-lock brks*. Writers also normally include *evaluative* segments, which consist of comments such as *like new*, *runs beautifully*, *must see*. A substantial majority (169, or 85%) of all 200 auto ads include both information types, with two thirds of these describing before evaluating (table 4.3). This is consistent with patterns of information sequencing described by Hoey (1983), who argues that just as the linguistic encoding of solutions tends to follow that of problems, the expression of an evaluative stance tends to follow actions. This is not to say that the dominant pattern cannot be reversed, and the language is rich in grammatical devices such as passivization that permit just such a reversal, typically for purposes of thematization or emphasis. But generally speaking, the sequencing of more factual, descriptive items before evaluative ones might be seen as most unmarked, a pattern also noted in journalistic language (Bell, 1991) and academic discourse (Swales, 1990).[11]

To summarize, a typical auto ad might be the following:

(76) 87 CADILLAC SEDAN DEVILLE.
Blue/blue leather interior. 49,000 mi.
Mint condition. $10,500. (213) 487-1234.

The information structure of this typical text might be represented schematically as shown in (table 4.4). In 12% of the cases, the

Table 4.3 Information content in the middle segment of auto ads

Information structure	No. of tokens	% of total
Descriptive, evaluative	130	65.0
Descriptive, not evaluative	39	19.5
Evaluative, descriptive	24	12.0
Evaluative, not descriptive	5	2.5
Others	2	1.0
Total	200	100.0

Table 4.4 Information sequencing in auto ads

Identifying	Descriptive	Evaluative	Transactional
87 Cadillac Sedan Deville	Blue/blue leather interior. 49,000 mi	Mint condition	$10,500. (213) 487-1234

inner pattern is reversed, however. Even more striking, a few ads omit altogether the dominant information type—the descriptive segment. This confirms that in CAR, as in most language use, a powerful convention need not be absolutely inflexible.

While placing description before evaluation may seem a natural ordering, no single pattern could be said to apply to the sequencing of individual items within the descriptive segment. Thus color, a feature mentioned in nearly half of all auto ads (91 out of 200), could presumably occur anywhere in a descriptive sequence. Yet in almost two-thirds of the cases, it occurs immediately after the identifying segments—that is, first in a series of descriptive items (table 4.5). In only a quarter of those auto ads that mention color does this segment come last in a descriptive sequence. Since the sequencing of information is largely free from editorial interference, this pattern confirms the fact that powerful conventions need not be overwhelming and that originality can always be accommodated within a dominant pattern of information sequencing.

Table 4.5 Location of color information in auto ads

Color occurs after	No. of tokens	% of total
Identifying	57	62.6
Identifying, descriptive	23	25.3
Identifying, evaluative	7	7.7
Others	4	4.4
Total	91	100.0

Apartment ads

Typically, an apartment ad opens with a main geographical *locator*: HOLLYWOOD HILLS; EAGLE ROCK /Glendale adjac. It invariably ends on a *transactional* element that contains the telephone number and required rent, mostly in that order, with—in roughly similar proportions to auto ads—an occasional mention of a contact name (20 tokens out of a total of 200 ads): *$435 mo + sec 213-254-1234; call Jim 213-392-1234*. Much of the ad is devoted to verifiable *descriptive* information: *1BR, parking, hardwood floors*.

In 88 (44%) out of a total of 200 ads, part of this segment can consist of additional geographical information beyond the basic location of the apartment:

(77) HOLLYWOOD, charming Spanish studio, 2 bdrm, formal dng rm <u>on North Ardmore bet Melrose & Santa Monica, W of Normandie,</u> $750 mo 213-665-1234

In contrast, this information complements the opening by being placed immediately after the principal locator in only 28 (16%) of the ads in this category. Some central segments also include preferences in the form of an *injunction*: This injunction occurs in 50 (25%) of all apartment ads, and it is placed before the final transactional segment of rent and telephone information in 39 (78%) of those 50 texts: *pet okay; no section 8; good credit a must*.

Many apartment ads also contain an *evaluative* element in the form of an overall comment, which can take a variety of forms: *must see; convenient; unusually interesting*. Most commonly, this element consists of a descriptive element modified by an adjective: *breathtaking views; elegant 2BR; quiet area*. Slightly over half (53%) of the ads in this category give descriptive information only (table 4.6).

In this ad category, no ads evaluate without describing. Yet of the 91 texts containing both descriptive and evaluative types of information, as many as 39 (43%) place evaluative segments before descriptive ones, a surprisingly high figure when compared to the reverse, presumably more unmarked, sequencing that predominates in auto ads.

Table 4.6 Information content in the middle segment of apartment ads

Information structure	No. of tokens	% of total
Descriptive only	106	53.0
Evaluative only	0	0
Both	91	45.5
Neither	3	1.5
Total	200	100.0

Typical of an apartment ad is the following text:

(78) WILSHIRE CENTER, lrg, 1 bdrm, upper, s&r, air, ceil fan, mini blinds & crpt, quiet cln bldg, sm pet ok, $510 mo 213-661-1234

The information structure of this ad is displayed in table 4.7.

In summary, a degree of variation in information sequencing in apartment ads does not obscure the fact that a substantial proportion of the data can be converted into a model to which less predictable cases of information sequencing can be compared. Overall, this constitutes additional evidence of the power of conventionalization in CAR.

Job ads

In this ad category, comments and evaluations are less frequent than in auto and apartment ads. This may be due to the wider range of

Table 4.7 Information sequencing in apartment ads

Location	(Geographical)	Descriptive	Evaluative	(Injunction)	Transactional
Wilshire Center		lrg. 1 bdrm, upper, s&r, air, ceil fan, mini blinds & crpt	quiet cln bldg	sm pet ok	$510 mo 213-661-1234

descriptive statements that need to be made about both actors and processes involved in offering, getting, and holding a job. The result is that those evaluative elements that are inserted tend to be interwoven with informational elements to form highly integrated nominal groups, which often include an attributive adjective:

(79) TELEMARKETING fund raising, day or eve
shift available, nice Hollywood office,
commission, bonus . . .

Job ads typically consist of five components. First is a *target* element, stating the type of person being recruited: *BILINGUAL RE intern position*; *PERSON friday*; *LEGAL secy*. Second, a *recruiter* element includes information about the company or individual placing the ad: *for flower shop*; *for up & coming writer*; *health & fitness industry*. It also gives details of the major duties of the job being advertised: *to handle scheduling*; *heavy phones*; *to drive private limo*; *no selling*. In about a third of cases, an indication of location is also given: *for a Pasadena clinic*; *hair studio in Beverly Hills*; *airport area*. Third is a *requirements* element, which specifies minimum qualifications or experience: *gd word processing skills*; *6 mo exp & a smile*; *no experience necessary*. Fourth, a *reward* element often includes benefits in addition to details of salary: *salaries to $105K*; *you're paid direct, $4.25–$6 hr*; *$2500 mo + benefits*. Finally, the ad contains a *contact* segment, usually consisting of a telephone number and, in about a quarter of the cases, a name: *call Mon–Sat 10am–3pm 213-731-1234*; *call Jean at 818-564-1234*.

Conventionalization strongly affects the placement of contact information, which occurs in the final position in 191 (96%) of a total of 200 ads. Location is mentioned in 65 ads, following the recruiter segment in 43 (66%) of those texts. Although there is greater variation in the endings, the most common pattern—that of reward followed by contact—is found in 80 (40%) of all the ads in this category (table 4.8). Conventionalization is also apparent in initial segments, which predominantly open with a reference to the target (table 4.9).

Characteristic of the overall pattern of information sequencing in this ad category is the following:

Table 4.8 Information sequencing in the final segment of job ads

Ending	No. of tokens	% of total
Reward, contact	80	40.0
Requirements, contact	49	24.5
Recruiter, contact	41	20.5
Locator, contact	21	10.5
Others	9	4.5
Total	200	100.0

(80) LEGAL secy, several positions in greater LA,
w recent exp in workman's comp or medical
malpractice, salary is $36,000 + xlnt benefits &
every 4th Friday off, call Lee Ann 213-385-1234

This prototypical pattern of information sequencing in job ads is represented in table 4.10.

Given the greater range of possible referents in job ads compared to auto and apartment ads, it is not surprising to find somewhat greater variation in information sequencing in this ad category, but this variation cannot obscure the conventionalized pattern that holds across many of these texts. Perhaps this recurrent pattern owes its strength to a concern for ease of processing. Or, as in Nair's (1992) comparison of Indian personal (matrimonial) ads with their closest American and British equivalents, it may be possible to link this pattern of information sequencing to the influence of an underlying Western ideology that favors the emphasis of individuals and titles and other social labels in preference to the larger organization for which these individuals might wish to work. Most probably, it is to

Table 4.9 Information focus in the initial segment of job ads

Opening	No. of tokens	% of total
Target	127	63.5
Recruiter	43	21.5
Requirements	16	8.0
Reward	14	7.0
Total	200	100.0

Table 4.10 Information sequencing in job ads

Target	Recruiter	Requirements	Reward	Contact
LEGAL secy	Several positions in greater LA	W recent exp in workman's comp or medical malpractice	Salary is $36,000 + xlnt benefits & every 4th Friday off	Call Lee Ann 213-385-1234

some combination of both types of influences that most texts in this ad category owe their overall form.

Personal ads

All personal ads include a *contact* segment that consists of at least a telephone or voice mail number: *(12345)*; *call #1234*; *Write with photo or call #1234*. This often follows a *location* segment: *SAN FERNANDO VALLEY (12345)*; *I am located in MONTEBELLO (12345)*.

Two other segments consist of a reference to *writer* and *reader*, respectively: <u>ASIAN lady, 36</u>, *wants* . . . ; <u>TALL, DARK, HANDSOME SJM, 26</u>, *seeks* . . . ; *SEEKING* <u>native American Indian male</u>; *LOOKING FOR* <u>MR. Green Card</u>.

Finally, personal ads often include a statement of *purpose*: *for fun, sharing, caring*; *who can show me CA*.

In her analysis of personal ads, Nair (1992) notes that American and British ads tend to emphasize the writer, leading to an active syntactic structure. In contrast, Indian openings focus on the readers, leading to passivization, and writers as agents of the search for a mate come last. Pursuing her search for social ideologies behind the linguistic conventions in her material, she argues that this pattern of information structure is a significant marker of cultural and ethnic identity, social and moral values, perceptions of self, and in particular the subservient position of individuals relative to family networks. The converse, she argues, is true in her corpus of Western texts.

In CAR, personal ads predominantly follow an active pattern of information sequencing, with writers overwhelmingly mentioned first. Rare exceptions consist of an opening *comment* on the interaction rather on the participants:

(81) <u>SEX CHANGE EXPERIMENT, just kidding</u>. Stable, cleancut, successful, handsome, DWM, 34, NS, seeks fun, adventure, long walks, dancing, conversation, laughter, you . . .

But fully 74% of all personal ads open with the writer segment. Moreover, writers are mentioned before readers in over four-fifths of the cases, regardless of the location of these two elements in the ad (table 4.11).

Mention of purpose is made in over half (115) of the 200 texts in this ad category. In 93 (82%) of the texts in which it appears, the purpose segment follows the writer-reader sequence, making this arrangement the dominant pattern in this category. Representative of this overall pattern is the following ad:

(82) SHF, leggy, very pretty, 30, brown eyes, blond, 5'2", sks SWM/DWM, blond, 25–41 for fun and who knows? I'm in INLAND EMPIRE (12345)

This typical text is represented in table 4.12.

As in the case of job ads, this dominant pattern of information sequencing may be explained at least in part by the social ideologies

Table 4.11 Information content in the middle segment of personal ads

Information structure	Total	%
Writer, reader	166	83.0
Reader, writer	25	12.5
Others	9	4.5
Total	200	100.0

Table 4.12 Information sequencing in personal ads

Writer	(Location)	Reader	Purpose	Contact
SHF, leggy very pretty, 30, brown eyes, blond, 5'2"		Sks SWM/DWM, blond, 25–41	For fun and who knows?	I'm in INLAND EMPIRE (12345)

that may—overtly or covertly—help shape it and give it its resilience. From this perspective, writers as principal agents in the search for a mate will tend to highlight themselves because the world into which they have been socialized values (or claims to value) action over acceptance and individual effort over institutional control and subservience to institutions and their representatives. Yet this is not to say that social conditioning is the only determining factor worthy of attention when attempting to account for language form and for information structure in particular. Instead, more tangible factors will need to be invoked to explain variations in form across different ad categories.

Summary

In discussing the role of conventionalization in CAR, I have noted the power of repetition and the strength of patterns of information sequencing in shaping language form. In reviewing these patterns, I have anticipated my discussion in chapter 5 of the impact of variation in functional circumstances on the linguistic form of each ad category represented in the CAR corpus.

To summarize my findings so far: auto ads allow limited variation in the sequencing of major information components, and their minimally elaborated texts make extensive use of editorially imposed abbreviations. Dispensable items such as intensifiers and adjectives are found along with coordinated pairs of verbs in rigid collocations. Yet collocational rigidity does not typically extend to articles, pronouns, or modals, which are often absent from what would be considered obligatory contexts in the literary grammar.

In contrast, apartment ads permit greater variation in information sequencing. Editorially imposed abbreviations function as short cuts and register markers, and the lexical range is relatively narrow and predictable. As in auto ads, collocational rigidity does not appear to cause the retention of features such as articles, pronouns, or modals in obligatory contexts, although the presence of some prepositions may be linked to the rigidity of the segments in which they appear.

Job ads tend to emphasize targets rather than writers, although a degree of variation is noticeable. Some texts include elaborated, non-register-specific idiomatic segments, as well as register-specific collocations of word types or word classes. Modals and negatives collocate with a small range of verbs and nouns, and the rigidity of idiomatic segments occasionally extends to articles.

Personal ads predominantly follow an active pattern of information sequencing. Syntactic elaboration is seen in idiomatic segments and quotations. Abbreviations operate as both short cuts and register markers. Frequent items tend to occur in predictable positions. Finally the rigidity of idiomatic segments can extend to articles but more often to negatives and prepositions, where they collocate with a small range of nouns in frequently recycled frames.

In summary, CAR shows signs of the conventionalization present throughout language as groups develop norms appropriate to each occasion and as users acquire and modify these norms. Prefabricated segments and predictable patterns of information sequencing are likely to be partly conditioned by the dominant ideologies of the culture in which they are used. Exactly how conventionalization and cognitive and functional factors combine to shape CAR is the focus of the final chapter of this book.

5
Functional variation

So far I have shown that despite the presence of prepatterned and prefabricated segments, what characterizes CAR texts above all other features is their minimal degree of syntactic elaboration. As a result, the notion of obligatory context cannot be applied to the measurement of syntactic elaboration in this register because attempts to identify missing features often amount to little more than guesswork. I also noted that the degree of syntactic elaboration appears to vary systematically across ad categories. That is, a variable proportion of the writer's limited resources will be spent on the function words that normally underpin recognizable syntactic structure and make the difference between parataxis and syntax. Since greater or lesser frequency of function words constitutes clear-cut evidence of greater or lesser syntactic elaboration, I now propose to quantify the frequency of function words in CAR. I will no longer compare this frequency with that in a wider corpus, such as *LOB* or *Brown*, but across the four categories in the CAR corpus. The question then is, Why do ad writers in one category aim for more elaborated syntax, or why do they systematically insert more or fewer function words in one category than in another? I will then have to offer an explanation for that variation in terms of some of the factors that may condition it.

The first step is to spell out the criteria used in selecting a set of features suitable for analysis. In studies of register variation in general, any given set of features constitutes a valid indicator of register differences provided the features within the set exhibit quantifiable covariation with the functional circumstances of the texts under scrutiny (Labov, 1969, 1972; Lavandera, 1978). This paradigm also requires sociolinguistic variables to be both referentially identical and contrastive in their social or stylistic distribution. In practice, sociolinguists have often been unwilling to extend the notion of sociolinguistic variables beyond phonological variation since only such features as dropped final consonants or reduced consonant clusters can be safely assumed to be of little or no semantic relevance.

This is an ideal that cannot be strictly adhered to if sociolinguistic analysis and especially the study of register variation are to gain in descriptive scope and explanatory power. It is true, as Cheshire (1987) points out, that the major contribution of Labovian linguistics has been to show that fluctuation in language use did not constitute free variation but could in fact be systematically linked to functional factors. Ideally, variations should be studied in experimental settings in which functional motivations are treated as independent variables and kept as constant as possible so that their possible effect on form can be examined under controlled conditions. However, the interplay between form and meaning is typically dynamic, nowhere more so than in the study of register variation, in which content cannot by definition be kept constant across registers. Thus, while a strict application of the Labovian paradigm may be theoretically attractive, the proposition cannot in practice be reconciled with the explication of register variation.

Still, variables should be kept as stable as the realities of language use permit. In CAR, this means that, in order to be selected for analysis, a variable has to carry as little referential meaning as possible. That is, it should operate primarily as a syntactic operator (or function word) rather than as a semantically charged item (or content word). It should appear in the corpus with sufficient frequency to permit statistical treatment. It should also conform to Biber's (1994) description of *register features* as core elements, distributed throughout the language in systematic co-occurrence patterns. These features contrast with *register markers*—such as the three-letter abbreviations of personal ads—which function as conventional indicators of a register but are too rare to be observable in systematic co-occurrence patterns in wider contexts.

Taking as a starting point my earlier description of the major linguistic features of CAR, I can describe lexical items such as nouns, adjectives, verbs, and adverbs as content words, which thus play no part in this attempt to quantify syntactic elaboration in CAR. Similarly, both negatives and modals come too close to semantic contentfulness to qualify. This leaves a set of six variables (henceforth *features*) that broadly meet the criteria. These consist of definite articles, indefinite articles, first and second person pronouns, relative pronouns, copulas, and—despite the fact that semantic neutrality varies somewhat within the class—prepositions.

Cross-category analysis of features

Definite articles

As reported in chapter 3, the definite article represents a far smaller proportion of word tokens in CAR than in the *LOB* and *Brown* corpora. However, a breakdown of these data reveals substantial variation in frequency across ad categories. (Refer to table 5.1 for frequency counts for each of the six features discussed in this chapter, in raw form and expressed as a percentage of the total.)[1] At one extreme are auto ads, with no tokens of definite articles at all. At the other are personal ads, in which tokens of the article represent 0.3% of all word tokens. This leaves apartment and job ads evenly distributed in between, with 0.1% and 0.2%, respectively, of the word tokens accounted for by definite articles.

In addition, the mean length of all ads containing the definite article (22.4 words per ad) is significantly greater (Mann Whitney p: <.02) than the mean length of all ads in the corpus (20.1 words per ad). (See table 5.2 for data on ad length for each of the six features discussed in this chapter.)[2] This suggests that writers who include the dispensable definite article in their ads do not do so by reducing the frequency of some other feature. Instead, they are prepared to produce a longer, possibly more expensive ad.[3] More specifically, greater mean length affects ads in the job category (23.0 words per ad) and the personal category (23.4 words per ad) most noticeably, although low numbers preclude any firm conclusions (Anova F: 2.78, p: <.08). The fact that this difference is on the margin of statistical significance constitutes a further indication of a pattern of systematic cross-category variation in the use of function words and in the degree of syntactic elaboration in CAR texts.

Table 5.1 Frequency of selected syntactic features in the CAR corpus

Ad category[a]	No. of words	Definite articles		Indefinite articles		Pronouns		Relative pronouns		Be copulas		Prepositions	
		N	%	N	%	N	%	N	%	N	%	N	%
Autos	3,573	0	0	1	0	0	0	0	0	0	0	37	1.0
Apartments	4,185	6	0.1	7	0.1	5	0.1	0	0	3	0.1	68	1.6
Jobs	4,002	10	0.2	23	0.6	27	0.7	3	0.1	29	0.7	169	4.2
Personals	4,315	14	0.3	39	0.9	99	2.3	20	0.5	52	1.2	157	3.6
All ads	16,075	30	0.2	70	0.4	131	0.8	23	0.1	84	0.5	431	2.7

[a]Total *n* in each category was 200, 100 from each newspaper.

Table 5.2 Length of ads containing selected syntactic features in the CAR corpus

Ad category	CAR corpus			Ads with definite articles				Ads with indefinite articles				Ads with pronouns			
	No. of Ads	Mean No. of words	SD	N	%	Mean no. of words	SD	N	%	Mean no. of words	SD	N	%	Mean no. of words	SD
Autos	200	17.9	5.3	0	0	0	0	1	0.5	20.0	0	0	0	0	0
Apartments	200	20.9	5.1	5	2.5	18.0	4.3	7	3.5	26.1	4.6	3	1.5	21.7	5.5
Jobs	200	20.0	5.3	8	4.0	23.0	6.2	20	10.0	23.3	4.7	22	11.0	22.1	4.5
Personals	200	21.6	2.4	12	6.0	23.4	3.7	35	17.5	22.4	4.7	59	29.5	22.6	2.5
All ads	800	20.1	4.9	25	3.1	22.4	5.1	63	7.9	23.1	3.8	84	10.5	22.4	3.2

	Ads with relative pronouns				Ads with *be* copulas				Ads with prepositions			
	N	%	Mean no. of words	SD	N	%	Mean no. of words	SD	N	%	Mean no. of words	SD
Autos	0	0	0	0	0	0	0	0	24	12.0	21.0	5.8
Apartments	0	0	0	0	3	1.5	24.7	2.5	55	27.5	24.1	5.8
Jobs	3	1.5	23.1	5.7	27	13.5	23.4	5.4	115	57.5	20.9	4.8
Personals	19	9.5	21.9	2.7	46	23.0	23.1	2.9	123	61.5	21.7	2.6
All ads	22	2.8	22.1	3.1	76	9.5	23.3	3.9	317	39.6	21.8	4.5

Indefinite articles

Although the shortfall is smaller than for the definite article, I showed earlier that indefinite articles represent a smaller proportion of word tokens in CAR than in *LOB* or *Brown*. While low numbers once again caution against generalization, the indefinite article use resembles that of its definite counterpart, with auto and apartment ads clustering at one extreme (0% and 0.1% of all word tokens, respectively) and job (0.6%) and personal ads (0.9%) at the other.

The picture is less clear concerning the mean length of ads containing the article since now apartment ads are longer. Yet insertion of the indefinite article into an ad correlates with a readiness to sacrifice brevity (23.1 words per ad versus 20.1 for the corpus as a whole; Mann Whitney p: <.01). Once again, the variation in mean ad length across ad categories comes close to statistical significance (Anova F: 3.01, p: <.06). However, the pattern of distribution across ad categories for the definite article is not repeated.

First and second person pronouns

While lower than in *LOB* and *Brown*, first and second person pronoun use in CAR is not as infrequent as observations of their relative rarity in other simple registers might have predicted.[4] What is also striking is the degree of variation across ad categories, which once again spreads along a continuum. First and second person pronouns never appear in auto ads and represent only 0.1% of all word tokens in apartment ads. In job ads, this figure rises sharply to 0.7%. But in personal ads, first and second person pronouns represent 2.3% of all word tokens, a figure that is well above both *LOB* (1.7%) and *Brown* (1.5%).

First and second person pronoun use also correlates with greater mean ad length (22.4 versus 20.1 words per ad for the corpus as a whole; Mann Whitney p: <.01). Here ad length follows the now familiar distribution along a continuum (autos, 0; apartments, 21.7; jobs, 22.1; personals, 22.6); however, the narrow spread of the variation and the low numbers in apartment ads combine to deny this observation any statistical significance (Anova F: .28, p: <.76).

Relative pronouns

The frequency of relative pronouns in CAR is less than that of both *LOB* and *Brown* and largely restricted to the relativization of subjects. However, relative pronouns appear overwhelmingly in personal ads, with the balance in job ads. Indeed, the frequency of the relative pronoun in personal ads (0.5% of all word tokens) approaches that of *LOB* and *Brown* (0.8%). However, auto and apartment ad writers avoid the feature altogether.

Given the concentration of relative pronouns in personal ads, it is not possible to compare ad categories for mean ad length. But the frequency of relative pronouns correlates significantly with longer ad length (22.1 words per ad compared to 20.1 for the CAR corpus as a whole; Mann Whitney p: <.03). In principle, any extra word will contribute to greater ad length. Indeed, I have shown that relative pronouns tend to occur in clauses in which the overall level of syntactic elaboration is relatively high and, therefore, costly. A possible consequence of this linguistic choice is that in return for some communicative advantage, a penalty might have to be paid in greater ad length. What the trade-off might be—that is, what might be gained from opting for the greater syntactic elaboration represented by relative pronouns and relative clauses—is a question that I address later in this chapter.

Be *Copulas*

Copula use in CAR is noticeably lower than in *LOB* and *Brown*, but as with the other features in the set, raw frequency counts mask a great deal of cross-category variation. Once again, variation is distributed along a continuum. Clustered at one end are auto ads with no tokens of *be* copulas at all and apartment ads in which *be* copulas represent just 0.1% of all word tokens. In contrast, the figure reaches 0.7% of word tokens in job ads and 1.2 % in personal ads. Thus despite spatial constraints, some writers are willing to pay in spatial terms the price of inserting a dispensable copula into their text.

Greater copula use also tends to correlate with greater ad length (23.3 words per ad rather than the 20.1 for the corpus as a whole; Mann Whitney p: <.01). However, differences in length across the three categories in which copulas appear are not statistically significant (Anova F: 0.25, p: <.78).

Prepositions

Based on the three most common types, namely, *with*, *for*, and *of*, preposition use in CAR is lower than in *LOB* and *Brown*, though the shortfall is less than the label of function word—with the assumption of dispensability that it carries—might predict. Here, too, the data reveal the earlier pattern of distribution ranging along a continuum, with auto ads (1.0% of all word tokens) and apartment ads (1.6%) at one extreme, and—albeit in reverse order—job ads (4.2%) and personal ads (3.6%) at the other.

Use of at least one of the three prepositions also correlates with greater mean length. Overall mean length reaches 21.8 words per ad rather than the 20.1 for the entire CAR corpus (Mann Whitney p: <.01). Significant variation in ad length is also found across ad categories (Anova F: 6.52, p: <.01). Yet it is difficult to explain the fact that apartment ads (24.1 words per ad) outstrip the other three categories, with their relatively narrow range of 20.9 to 21.7 words per ad only.

Patterns of distribution

Taken as a whole, it is clear that the low frequency of function words is a major characteristic of CAR. To be sure, these data reinforce a sense of what Ferguson calls an "overall family resemblance" (1983, p. 160) between CAR and other simple registers, an observation that he bases on his typology of common features of simple registers (reproduced in appendix A). In other words, CAR writers and users of other simple registers share a tendency to keep the frequency of function words low. In an attempt to explain this commonality, it has been claimed that pressure to keep language simple for whatever purpose—to communicate with an infant or a foreigner, or to save time or space—may encourage the encoder to fall back intuitively on a universal linguistic core (Samarin, 1971; Ferguson, 1982). Thus, despite some fundamental differences among simple registers in terms of their functional characteristics, they may share some of their features because human beings are innately equipped with a shared sense of how to dispense with unnecessarily elaborated syntax whenever that is appropriate.

This is not to deny that the optimal mode of expression for each communicative situation must to a large extent be learned. Ad writers commonly report looking at recent ads before copying what they see as an appropriate style in a given publication. But while learned behavior may be especially useful in explaining the linguistic form of classified ads, it does not account for the striking similarities noted across a range of simple registers, including this one.

A more serious problem with positing an innate sense of what is available for omission under certain circumstances as the major factor in shaping the form of simple registers is that we should expect those dispensable items that do occur to be uniformly distributed across comparable text types. Here, this means that the frequency of these items should be roughly constant across the four ad categories since texts are uniformly constrained by the spatial limitations of a conventional ad. However, a closer look at the frequency of the present set of six features as a percentage of its frequency in *LOB* and *Brown* combined shows substantial variation. At one extreme, the frequency of definite articles reaches only 2.8% of its level in *LOB* and *Brown*; at the other extreme, the frequency of prepositions reaches 42.5%, while the remaining four features cluster between 11.8% and 17.7% (table 5.3). Given this level of variation, function words simply cannot be lumped together. Clearly, the frequency of function words as an indicator of the level of syntactic elaboration is determined by other factors, which need to be uncovered.

In addition, a cognitive hypothesis of a possibly innate sense of what constitutes linguistic simplicity will only hold if no systematic variation is found across ad categories. The data, however, show the opposite to be true (table 5.4). What these data reveal is that to the extent that these features are used, their frequency ranges systematically along a continuum. At one end are auto and apartment ads, with 10.6 and 21.3 tokens of all six features per 1,000 words, respectively; at the other end are job and personal ads, with 65.2 and 88.3 tokens, respectively. As soon as the numbers rise sufficiently to provide some noticeable differentiation in their bar graph repre-

Table 5.3 Frequency of selected syntactic features per 1,000 words

Feature	CAR	LOB	Brown	CAR as % of LOB-Brown
Definite articles	1.9	68.3	68.1	2.8
Indefinite articles	4.4	25.4	26.3	17.0
Pronouns	8.4	71.4	70.3	11.8
Relative pronouns	1.4	8.1	7.6	17.7
Be copulas	5.2	36.4	32.5	15.1
Prepositions	36.5	87.0	85.8	42.5

sentation, the four ad categories tend to cluster in pairs, with auto and apartment ads at one end of the continuum and job and personal ads at the other.

Confirmation of this distribution comes from data on patterns of co-occurrence of the six features across the CAR corpus. It is possible that ads at the job and personal end of the continuum reach higher levels of syntactic frequency of the six features under study because of a relatively small number of ads that use an abnormally high number of tokens. In other words, the presence of just a few deviant ads that exhibit perhaps extravagant wordings or levels of elaboration atypical of this register might be sufficient to explain the distribution. What the data reveal, however, is that patterns of co-occurrence closely parallel those noted in the overall distribution of the features (table 5.5). Roughly half of all the ads make no use of any of the features, but this figure once again masks a great deal

Table 5.4 Frequency of selected syntactic features per 1,000 words, by ad category

Ad category	Total no. of words	Frequency (%)					
		Definite articles	Indefinite articles	Pronouns	Relative pronouns	*Be* copulas	Prepositions
Autos	3,573	0	.3	0	0	0	10.4
Apartments	4,185	1.4	1.7	1.2	0	0.7	16.2
Jobs	4,002	2.5	5.7	6.7	0.7	7.2	42.2
Personals	4,315	3.2	9.0	22.9	4.6	12.1	36.3

Table 5.5 Percentage of ads that contain 0 to 6 of the selected syntactic features

Ad category	No. of features in ad						
	0	1	2	3	4	5	6
Autos	86.0	14.0	0	0	0	0	0
Apartments	65.5	32.0	1.5	0.5	0.5	0	0
Jobs	34.5	40.5	18.5	5.0	1.5	0	0
Personals	20.0	41.5	21.5	12.5	3.5	1.0	0
All ads	51.5	32.0	10.3	4.5	1.4	0.3	0

of variation. At one end of the continuum, a high proportion of auto and apartment ads (86% and 65.5%, respectively) use none of the six features. At the other, the figures drop to 34.5% for job ads and 20% for personal ads. Moreover, there are more ads in the job and personal categories that use at least one feature (jobs, 40.5%; personals, 41.5%) than there are those using no feature at all. Finally, in both of these categories, a higher number of feature types is likely to be used in a single ad. While auto ad writers never include more than one of the six features in their texts, 3.5% of personal ads include as many as four.

It is true that an alternative reading of the data may focus on the fact that roughly half the texts in the corpus contain no tokens of the six features. Thus it may be argued that a substantial section of the corpus has been ignored. But while this subset may be the focus of valuable further research, this distribution does not invalidate the finding that to the extent that they use any of the features in question, ad writers do not distribute them uniformly across text types.

So far I have presented data that confirm that uniformly stringent spatial constraints do not lead to uniformly weak syntactic elaboration. Constructing a text within narrow spatial constraints cannot simply be a matter of choosing, consciously or not, between function and content words, eliminating the former and retaining the latter. Instead, variation in the degree of syntactic elaboration as measured by the frequency of functions words varies systematically across ad categories. This suggests that the degree of elaboration covaries with the communicative function that these text types are meant to perform. To be sure, part of the production of simple language may well be traced to the operation of a possibly innate sense of what to omit in a spatially constrained text, but this hypothesis has been shown to be inadequate in accounting fully for the powerful pattern of variation in syntactic elaboration in CAR. The search for the functional parameters of this pattern thus becomes the next focus of this discussion.

Functional analysis

Whenever participants are spatially distant and writing becomes the most convenient and most likely medium of communication, the degree of syntactic elaboration of texts should be conditioned primarily by the editing process that writing affords. That is, the level of syntactic elaboration is expected to be high because the writer normally has few spatial constraints to deal with and ample opportunity—whenever appropriate—to integrate information into complex sentences. In the case of CAR texts, spatial constraints on the production of ads of a comparable type are roughly constant across ad categories, although the degree of elaboration varies systematically. The challenge therefore is to relate variation in the form of these ads to variation in the linguistic purpose that this form is meant to serve.

The response is to see the components of syntactic structure, including the six features under study, not just as cogs in the syntactic machinery but as the writer's reaction to circumstances of production, shaping individually and collectively the linguistic fulfillment of specific communicative purposes. Assuming that communicative purpose also influences the selection and frequency of items normally dispensable in a simple register, I must now investigate the strategic function of each of the six features in the set to explain in functional terms any systematic relationship that may hold the between the presence of that feature and the communicative purpose. Thus each of the six features in the set must be tested for possible functional justifications along one or more dimensions. Any feature whose presence can be attributed to that dimension can be said to have been accounted for. Any feature that cannot be accounted for in this manner requires another dimension to be added to the model, until each of the six features has been accounted for in functional terms.

This is not to say that variation in communicative purpose alone explains variation in the frequency of the six function words under consideration. As I have argued, variation in the frequency of some of these function words may be a consequence of variation in the frequency of other word categories—frequency of articles covarying with noun use, for example. However, my primary concern here is no longer the syntagmatic relations that tie discourse together, often in highly conventionalized patterns, but the functional parameters of linguistic form.

So far I have given priority to the identification and quantification of patterns of systematic variation in the data before deriving a hypothesis for their explanation. At this point, the analysis must acquire what Biber calls an "interpretive" nature (1988, p. 92), in the sense that the validity of each of the dimensions needed for a full account of the variation in the data depends on the most widely accepted communicative function of each feature, a task not easily amenable to quantitative methods.

Definite articles

Summarizing from chapter 3, we note that Hawkins (1978, 1990) discusses the dual role of the English definite article, which functions as an endophoric marker, referring the decoder to information that is given because it appears explicitly in current discourse. But the definite article also marks exophoric, or associative, reference. In this role, the article is not explicitly related to any previous discourse, and assessment of the relevance of the noun phrase it introduces is largely the responsibility of the decoder. This makes the article a highly hearer-sensitive feature. As such, it is likely to be found in texts where comprehension depends on having access to a complex system of semantic and contextual associations.

Given the spatial constraints of CAR, is not likely that a definite article will be needed to introduce repeated references to the same concept or entity in any ad category. Yet this study shows that the frequency of the definite article use is not uniform across ad categories. At one extreme, auto and apartment ads consist overwhelmingly of strings of items, each mentioned only once. At the other extreme, job and personal ads include segments that unambiguously invite insertion of a definite article. In addition, the actual frequency of the article is also higher in these two ad categories.

The most likely explanation for this variation is the considerable difference in the range of possible referents and the varying need to appeal to contextual associations. At one extreme, auto and apartment ads tend to refer exclusively to the components of the item being advertised. The very fact that, say, *alarm* or *kitchen* is mentioned in an auto or an apartment ad makes the relevance of these items to the whole message unambiguous:

(1) 87 BMW 325 Excellent condition.
   Black, 2 dr, auto, 60,000 mi, <u>alarm</u>,
   fully loaded, factory stereo, well-
   maintained. $9200. Call . . .

(2) HOLLYWOOD, single, <u>kitchen</u> bar, c&d, air,
   sec bldg, lndry, prkng, $450 mo . . .

As a result writers can take greater risks with underspecification, confident in the belief that a cooperative, informed reader will correctly identify referents and their key associations from within a narrow range of possibilities.

Job and personal ad writers, in contrast, have to refer to a much greater range of entities, functions, contextual factors, and relevant shared knowledge, all within narrow spatial constraints. Far from representing a squandering of resources in a spatially constrained register, inserting into a text a segment headed by a relatively dispensable definite article may in fact be a highly efficient strategy for referring to one of a multiplicity of possible referents while hinting at a large chunk of shared context:

(3) LEGAL secretary trainee, type 75, dictaphone,
   some word processing & a desire to learn
   legal work for one interesting attorney who
   will train <u>the right person</u>, benefits & bonuses,
   $2000 mo . . .

(4) ATHLETIC, TALL, ROMANTIC
guy, 20, who flunked disco and bars
seeks attractive, slender, affec-
tionate female, 18–23 for <u>the usual
reasons</u>. Call . . .

It is true that, as in all language use, comprehension of an auto or an apartment ad also requires that some background be shared between participants. But this is limited to a common awareness of what makes the object of the transaction distinctive. Little or nothing is said or even hinted at that might refer to the participants themselves. In job and personal ads, however, detailed specification of the information introduced by the definite article could not possibly be fitted into the spatial constraints of the ad. Thus only individuals with inside knowledge of what constitutes *the right person* for the job or *the usual reasons* for entering into a relationship can hope to recover the intended reference. This kind of knowledge depends not only on the possession of *information* but also—crucially—on interpersonal *involvement*, and it is available only to those who have interacted with similar individuals in a similar context and who are willing to again interact in similar fashion. Given the substantially higher frequency of definite articles in job and personal ads than in auto and apartment ads, their distribution in CAR can be linked to one major communicative function, which, following Biber (1988), I label *involved* versus *informational*.

Indefinite articles

While the definite article presents an item as uniquely identifiable (Hawkins, 1978, 1990), its indefinite counterpart simply fails to present it as defined (Huddleston, 1984). The referent may well turn out to be the only exemplar of its type, although in most cases this is unlikely. In practice, indefinite article use is likely to correlate with the presentation of information about unique items mentioned only once. This should make its presence more likely in auto and apartment ads, which tend to consist of strings of content words, most of them nouns. Yet in the CAR corpus, its use has been found to be substantially higher in job and personal ads, which are characterized by greater involvement between participants.

(5) STUNNING SAF, 28, sks <u>a gorgeous, smart, romantic, successful, outrageous, SWM</u> who can make me laugh. Photo pls . . .

(6) HAIRSTYLIST, ELECTROL-
OGIST, MANICURIST for <u>a new full service beauty salon</u>. Larchmont Village. Ask for Nili or Genevieve . . .

Certainly, a need for explicitness cannot be invoked since the morphologically transparent singularity of most nouns and the presence of rich contextual clues makes indefinite articles largely redundant. Once again, this leaves the notion of interpersonal involvement as the most likely cause of the relatively high frequency of indefinite articles in job and personal ads. Here, anticipation of interpersonal involvement may make the notion of self-image central to the production of job and personal ads. This may lead writers in the direction of more sophisticated, that is, more elaborated, language. On occasion, a preoccupation with a personal or corporate image may well encourage the retention of relatively dispensable indefinite articles in recycled segments:

(7) FRONT office medical lt accurate typing, 6
mo exp <u>& a smile</u>, join friendly general
practice clinic, no uniforms, promotable,
salary-wise, interesting position, benefits &
prkng $1500 mo . . .

As I showed in the case of definite articles, these segments may not only refer to a kind of shared knowledge that is dependent on the possession of information about a proposed transaction, but also, and more important, hint at past and future interpersonal involvement. That is, they signal that intended readers are meant to have both the personal experience of similar interactions and the willingness to interact once again along similar lines.

First and second person pronouns

In Halliday & Hasan's (1976) analysis of personal reference in English, the role of personal pronouns is to define individuals in terms of their respective roles in the communicative process. Chafe (1985) points out that a language user is typically concerned, in addition to establishing personal deixis and delivering propositional content, with the presentation of the self, leading to first person pronoun use, as well as with the dynamics of the interaction, leading to second person pronoun use. Ferguson argues that the pronominal system is particularly susceptible to register shifts, which mark "changes in situational context or in interactants' purposes, attitudes, or communicative strategies" (1982, p. 52). Thus it is likely that first and second person pronoun use will be more frequent in contexts in which prolonged interpersonal involvement is expected beyond some initial transaction. Cases of this usage are occasionally found in apartment and job ads but mostly in personal ads:

(8) HOLLYWOOD. We make deals.
    Beautiful new building. Central
    air/heat. Fireplace, Jacuzzi, gated
    parking. Friendly manager ...

(9) OBERON & Naomi are seeking fabulous,
    glamorous, bizarre, extraordinary, artists for
    up & coming club, any talent or tricks
    welcome, you get xlnt film & industry
    exposure ...

(10) UNCONVENTIONAL man, goodlooking,
     wants to melt your heart. Discover your
     mind, explore the world. Relax, say yes ...

Indirect confirmation of this interpretation comes from Biber's (1988) study of the distribution of 67 features across 23 written and spoken genres, in which first and second person pronouns are found to cluster, in texts of a mostly interactive nature, with—among others—demonstrative pronouns, stranded prepositions, and *that* deletions. The types of texts in which the frequency of personal pronouns tends to be high include spontaneous speeches and face-to-face conversations. This pattern contrasts with prepared speeches and academic prose, in which it is low.

However, it is not the case that all tokens of the indefinite article in this corpus can be accounted for in terms of a single dimension ranging from involved to informational functions. Nor should each token be linked to that single dimension only. Instead, it should be noted that contextual clues cannot always be relied upon to disambiguate the participants in an interaction. In auto and apartment ads, the focus of information is very much on just that, autos and apartments, with the role of writers and readers commonly understood and in no need of further specification. In contrast, job and personal ads must somehow make clear not only relevant issues such as working conditions or common interests but also which of the two sides involved in the proposed interaction—employer and employee or writer and reader as potential partners—is expected to do what. As a result, first or second person pronouns may need to be inserted in the interest of greater explicitness:

(11) TELEMARKETERS wtd, possible commission
of $375 day, huge demand, <u>customers call you</u>
for job directories, 1pm–6pm—call Mike
1pm–6pm . . .

(12) AFRICAN male, 36, 5'11", 190, sks lady
any race for serious relationship. <u>I like
cooking, sports, reading</u>. Letter/photo . . .

Thus a second dimension needs to be invoked to fully account for first and second person pronoun use in CAR. Once again, I follow Biber (1988) in labeling this additional dimension *implicitness* versus *explicitness*.

Relative pronouns

As I have noted, Pawley & Syder (1983a) and Fox & Thompson (1990) view relativization as a major area of differentiation between the vernacular and literary grammars of the language. They argue that it is the operation of real-time constraints that forces the vernacular grammar to relativize in ways often unnoticed or unrecognized by analysts of the literary grammar. Conversely, the typically written circumstances of the literary grammar typically allow for greater integration of components within a complex sentence (Ochs, 1979).[5]

In the minimally elaborated texts of auto and apartment ads, additional information regarding the focus of the ad is typically given in the form of a long series of uncoordinated descriptive or evaluative items. Here, referential attribution is nonproblematic. Writers expect readers to be aware of the relevance of, say, a "pullout stereo" to a "Volkswagon" [sic] or a "carpet" to a "2BR" apartment. In return, informed and cooperative readers must be willing to make the connection for themselves, and judging by the ubiquitousness of these ads, presumably they are:

(13) 81 VOLKSWAGON RABBIT. Convertible. White. <u>Pullout, stereo</u>, low miles—51,000, special rims, economy, super clean in & out. $3700 . . .

(14) BRENTWOOD, $945 2BR 2BA. 2 miles to UCLA, <u>carpet</u>, appliances. parking, laundry. Open daily 8am–5pm . . .

This extremely narrow range of possible referents permits the widespread underspecification that is characteristic of these texts, with little risk of referential misassignment. In contrast, writers of job and personal ads may have to disambiguate between a wider and potentially unpredictable range of referents, as well as between a correspondingly large number of possible connections between them:

(15) LEGAL secretary trainee, type 75, dictaphone, some word processing & a desire to learn legal work for one interesting attorney <u>who will train the right person</u>, benefits & bonuses, $2000 mo . . .

In these texts, relativization plays a direct part in providing greater explicitness and enabling readers to assign additional information correctly—in this case who will give the training and who will receive it. Thus, as with first and second person pronouns, the frequency of relative pronouns in job and personal ads can be linked to implicitness versus explicitness. This interpretation is supported by Biber's (1988) analysis, in which relativization of the subject position forms part of a cluster of features of greater explicitness, as in official documents or business letters. This contrasts with such texts as face-to-face and telephone conversations, in which contextual clues are normally sufficient.

Given the wealth of integrated alternatives at the writer's disposal, however, elaborated relative clauses may also play a part in indexing nonpropositional content. In texts in which only one referent is mentioned or at least highlighted, there is little or no risk of referential misassignment and therefore little or no need for the explicitness provided by a relativization:

(16) RICH woman <u>who loves travelling & clubbing</u> wants to share romance with attractive man. Please send photo . . .

The dimension from involved to informational functions may also help explain the presence of otherwise highly dispensable language in a spatially constrained register. As I argued in the case of definite and indefinite articles, job and personal ads suggest a much higher degree of anticipated interactional involvement between the writer and the reader. Here, the presentation of the self can be assumed to be of greater concern. This may encourage some writers to couch their message in relatively elaborated language, certainly beyond what could be expected—especially in a spatially constrained register—if their major communicative purpose was primarily informational.

This is not to say that the form of any one text must be shaped by one or the other of the two dimensions I propose. Few, if any, phenomena are due to single causes. Thus it should not be surprising to find both dimensions occasionally interacting in the same text and giving rise to two parallel structures for altogether different reasons, as in the following:

(17) GOODLOOKIN' REDHEAD SJF
<u>who has God directing her show,</u>
seeks SJM, 35–43 <u>who's also a long-term friend of Bill W's</u>. Call . . .

Here, the first relative pronoun can be regarded as superfluous since only one antecedent has so far been mentioned. Clearly, the writer had at her disposal a range of alternatives, not least a shorter, more integrated prepositional phrase. Thus the high level of syntactic elaboration should probably be linked not to a need for explicitness but to a concern with the presentation of the self and interpersonal involvement. The second relative pronoun, together with the inflected copula, introduces information that could be interpreted as referring to either of the two possible antecedents. Here, a concern with explicitness probably explains the pronoun's presence in this text.

Be *Copulas*

Although Labov (1969) shows that copulas can be a strong indicator of social differentiation, social factors are not likely to explain the distribution of this feature in CAR, for reasons that I have already reviewed. More relevant is the widespread absence of copulas in the writing of note-takers, produced under great pressure to condense (Janda, 1985). A more integrated alternative to copulas exists in the form of adjectives in attributive position (adj N) (Biber, 1988). This is more likely to be found in exchanges of a strongly informational nature, typically in highly planned written form. In contrast, predicative constructions (N *be* adj) tend to be more frequent in relatively unplanned, more fragmented discourse such as the language of sports announcers (Ferguson, 1983; Ghadessy, 1988; Romaine, 1994).

Copulas occur only rarely in CAR, although the corpus is rich in segments that call for the insertion of a copula in an expanded version of the text:

(18) HOLLYWOOD, come join the Hollywood
Royal apts, <u>now renting</u> sgls & 1 bdrms, $250
sec dep, $450–575 mo . . .

(19) AIRLINES <u>HIRING Immediate</u>,
entry level customer service, flight
attendants, clerical and maintenance. Excellent salaries and travel
benefits. Call . . .

When copulas do occur, mostly in job and personal ads, they invariably appear in ads that show signs of greater syntactic elaboration, co-occurring with other function words such as prepositions, modals, pronouns, and articles:

(20) ADMINISTRATIVE assistant, type 75, gd word
processing skills, <u>will be right hand</u> to to
person in company, able to make decisions,
grow with company, vy gd benefits, pckg,
retirement & free prkng, $2100 mo . . .

(21) <u>I am attractive</u>, intelligent, single,
black male, 40, seeking an intelligent
single attractive female, for mate . . .

This pattern exists despite the fact that the copula fulfills little of an essential semantic role since its two primary functions—the marking of tense and number—can easily be inferred from the context. Thus it makes little or no additional contribution to the level of explicitness of these messages.

Once again, this highly dispensable item is found to occur more frequently in texts whose authors can reasonably expect a greater degree of interpersonal involvement between themselves and a reader. Support for this interpretation comes from Biber's (1988) factorial distribution, which finds *be* as main verb clustering with features such as first and second person pronouns in texts strongly suggestive of interpersonal involvement like interviews or personal letters.[6] However, this conclusion should be qualified since, on closer analysis, 26 of the 84 tokens of copulas in the CAR corpus are in the infinitive following a modal:

(22) 10 SALES people wtd for outside sales job,
$2000–$6000 potential commission a month,
<u>can be full or part time</u>, selling educational
products . . .

In addition, half of these tokens are accounted for by the single collocation of the *be* infinitive following the modal *must*, overwhelmingly in job ads:

(23) DRIVERS wtd for airport shuttle to
Disneyland, <u>must be 25+</u>, reg or class 2 lic
both accepted, <u>must be honest</u>—call . . .

As I have argued, the saliency and relative frequency of these prefabricated segments may be due in part to processing advantages derived from the recycling of familiar patterns, which, in addition to being readily available, operate as both conveyors of meaning and markers of register. Yet a psycholinguistic interpretation is not incompatible with a functional one, especially since a degree of competition between functional factors is precisely what is implied by multidimensional accounts of register variation in general and of linguistic simplicity in particular.

Prepositions

Chafe (1982) lists the class of prepositions as one of a number of features that play an important role in integrating large amounts of information into what he calls *idea units*. Biber (1988) also notes that prepositions tend to co-occur with features of integrated, typically written discourse such as nominalizations and passives, mostly in texts of an informational or expository nature like journalistic writing or official documents. In CAR also, there are numerous examples of the ability of writers to pack information densely. Often, prepositional phrases play a crucial role in this process:

(24) SBM, 45, slightly disabled, cleancut,
sks SBF, 40–50, <u>for intimate friendship</u> &
<u>1 on 1</u> companionship, <u>into low stress</u>.
LOS ANGELES (12345)

(25) FULL TIME DRIVER <u>with reliable
vehicle</u> wanted <u>for weekday deliver-
ies</u>. Must be pleasant self-starter
<u>with a knowledge of the greater Los
Angeles area</u>. Call Glen <u>at (310) 936-1234</u>

In Biber's (1988) factorial distribution, prepositions tend to cluster with such features as nouns, high type-to-token ratio, and attributive adjectives in a pattern that he interprets as denoting the informational nature of the texts in which they occur, such as academic prose or press reportage. Biber's evidence comes from a large number of written and spoken sources covering a multiplicity of communicative purposes. However, this evidence only presents the aggregate tendency of prepositions to correlate with other features of mainly informational texts. When text types are examined individually, as they are here, systematic differentiation becomes apparent. At one extreme, auto and apartment ads deal with a relatively narrow semantic field in which relations between entities are so much a part of a shared context—as between *four cylinders* and a *Buick*, for example—that they need not be mentioned explicitly:

(26) 86 <u>BUICK</u> SKYLARK, 1 owner, auto, 46M, <u>4 cyl</u>,
cass radio, new front tires, $6000 . . .

In these texts mere listing appears to satisfy readers in their search for a reasonable match between the items in a list and their own understanding of how these items are supposed to interrelate. In contrast, writers and readers of job and personal ads have to cope with a much greater range of possible referents. At this end of the continuum, relations between entities often have to be made explicit because there may not be enough in the shared context to help readers predict which of a multiplicity of possible referential assignments is intended for the nouns in the prepositional phrase, as in the following:

(27) HIGHLY STRUNG, BEAUTIFUL
WF, vixen needs brave, affluent
handsome WM keeper (with spare
golden cage) to tame her wicked
ways. Call #1234

Thus I see variation in the need for explicitness as the primary factor behind preposition use in CAR, in addition to the collocational demands of specific lexical choices, which I discussed earlier.

It is possible in principle to test the notion that prepositions are crucial to the successful encoding of intratextual relations. I might test this by dropping all prepositions from a selection of ads from the CAR corpus and somehow measuring any change in clarity from the original versions in the expression of relations between referents. But apart from some major methodological problems inherent in attempts to measure such slippery notions as linguistic complexity and clarity, the difficulty is that the exercise would come uncomfortably close to the suggestion that producing simple language consists essentially of deleting nonessential segments from more elaborated underlying structures. Since I argue that it is far from axiomatic that deletion plays a central role in achieving linguistic simplicity, it is not clear that much would be learned in the process.

Instead, it may be more revealing to return to the role played by prefabricated chunks in the distribution of prepositional phrases in CAR. Preposition use does appear to be influenced to some extent by the collocational demands of specific lexical choices. It also reflects the need to encode explicitly the more complex semantic relations that exist between parties involved in a professional or romantic partnership than the predictability of those in auto and apartment contexts. The interplay between these and other factors is at the heart of the notion of a multifunctional model of linguistic simplification.

Discussion and implications

As in all language use, the nature of CAR texts reflects the complementary and sometimes conflicting factors that condition their composition. In this chapter, I have shown that CAR texts fall broadly into two groups, with auto and apartment ads at one end of a continuum and job and personal ads at the other. Essentially, these groups differ in their form in terms of their degree of elaboration as measured by the frequency of a set of function words.

At this point, it is worth noting that the corpus presents a second, equally systematic pattern, which governs the distribution of abbreviations and codes in these texts. Here, abbreviations are most frequent in auto and apartment ads, accounting for 27.3% and 29.2%, respectively, of all word tokens in these two ad categories.[7] In contrast, their frequency reaches only 16.5% and 10.2% of word tokens in job ads and personal ads, respectively. This correlates inversely with the frequency of the set of six features across ad categories at a level that is both very high and statistically significant (r^2: −.948, p: >.03, two-tailed) (table 5.6). This inverse correlation between the frequency of abbreviations and the degree of elaboration confirms that elaboration in CAR can be linked to the location of each text along two dimensions: the greater or lesser need for explicitness and the greater or lesser expectation of interpersonal involvement. That is, job and personal ad writers are more likely than auto and apartment ad writers to make explicit some of the less predictable referential links that exist between entities in their texts or between their texts and the outside world.

In addition, often correlating with a need for greater explicitness is a high type-to-token ratio (Biber, 1988). That is, the greater the range of possible referents, the greater the number of different word types that will figure in a text. For a given number of tokens a text tending toward greater explicitness will contain a higher number of

Table 5.6 Abbreviations and selected syntactic features as percentage of word tokens

Ad category	No. of words	Abbreviations		Features	
		N	%	N	%
Autos	1,672	456	27.3	20	1.2
Apartments	2,137	625	29.2	44	2.1
Jobs	2,077	343	16.5	132	6.4
Personals	2,147	219	10.2	168	7.8

types. Conversely, texts of roughly equal length that contain fewer referents or take many contextual features for granted will tend to rely on fewer word types. Here, type-to-token ratios for auto and apartment ads cluster closely in the 0.30 to 0.31 range. In contrast, personal ads and, especially, job ads show greater lexical variety (0.37 to 0.45, respectively) (refer back to table 4.2). This constitutes additional evidence that a need for greater explicitness is a major factor behind the substantially greater frequency of the six features in the job and personal ad categories.

However, the use of features whose absence would normally characterize simple registers also appears to be connected to the degree of expected interactional involvement between the ad writer and the reader. The suggestion of a dimension stretching from involved to informational functions does not, of course, claim to reflect the ad writer's deeper intent. Most certainly, I do not wish to imply that individual writers' deeper motivations can always be reliably divined from the form of their texts. Perhaps some advertisers regard transactions over an auto or an apartment as an emotional experience. Conversely, there is no reason to suppose that all prospective employers or romantic partners are as personally or emotionally motivated as their texts might suggest. The claim is simply that ad writers are aware of the need to present a specific face in a given communicative situation. Regardless, perhaps, of deeper motivations, they respond to the demands of the situation by putting their message in an appropriate, culturally sanctioned form.

In summary, the stringent spatial constraints under which CAR operates predict that classified ad writers should concentrate on essential referential information. An additional assumption is that writers will want their rationed linguistic resources to be put to maximal use and that relationships between entities should be made explicit only when absolutely necessary. Yet as Beaman (1984) notes, the higher the frequency of a feature—such as a coordinating conjunction—in a text, the less referential and the more indexical its load is likely to be—an observation which there is no reason not to extend to the frequency of function words in a simple register such as CAR. Thus the relatively frequent presence in some ad categories of features normally absent from a simple register suggests that, like language users in general, CAR writers are sensitive to variation in the need for explicitness and that they are both willing and able to signal potential interactional involvement with readers. This is an important finding in that it belies assumptions of uniformity and lack of communicative sophistication in the linguistic form of simple registers.

6

Classified advertising in its linguistic context

At the outset, I proposed to consider the nature of linguistic simplification. To do this, I examined a corpus of classified ads for evidence of the effect of spatial constraints on the syntactic structure of this simple register. I provided a description of the CAR corpus, and I showed that the register bypasses many of the syntactic requirements of the literary grammar, which typically controls written registers. I considered the spread of conventionalized register markers such as abbreviations, and I noted a widespread reliance on prefabricated segments, which were seen as reflecting the conventions of medium, location, and time. I noted that identical spatial constraints do not have a uniform effect on the degree of syntactic elaboration of CAR texts, and I showed that cross-category variation should be linked to differences in the impact of two key functional factors, namely, a varying need for explicitness and varying expectations of interactional involvement.

I now turn to the impact of these findings on some key issues that underlie discussions of the nature of linguistic simplicity. I begin by examining the value of my initial model of linguistic simplicity, which relied on a distinction between handicap and economy registers and between reduced and elaborated outputs, and I propose a refinement of the model. I then discuss the validity of an innateness hypothesis, which emphasizes cross-linguistic patterns of omission of dispensable features. I also consider some possible causes for the extensive presence of conventionalized and prefabricated segments in CAR. I challenge some of the theoretical assumptions that influence the study of language in context, in particular of register variation. Finally, I outline some possible directions of future research.

Toward a multifunctional model of linguistic simplicity

Description

Early in this book I reviewed a range of simple registers in terms of a three-way classification based on key functional parameters: handicap, economy, and social distancing. But in all language use, it is in combination, not individually, that these factors shape each specific register. That is, the users of any one simple register may well be responding to pressures for economy in a situation in which both linguistic limitations and social distancing are playing a part, and it is unlikely that any register can be described purely in terms of only one of these three labels. If so, this initial set of three discrete parameters cannot capture the complex network of constraints and motivations that underlie each simple register and give it its distinctive form.

In response, the following model aims to free the description of simple registers from the constraints of overspecific labeling. In his casting of sociolinguistic inquiry in Popperian terms, Janicki (1990) stresses that definitions should be seen as fuzzy labels, which have a better chance of reflecting the nature of any given concept than approaches claiming to uncover a set of properties that applies uniquely to it and distinguishes it from its neighbors. Thus the model I now propose allows for all 11 registers I reviewed earlier to be distinguished on the basis of at least one functional factor—that is, a variable that is likely to play a substantial role in shaping the register, while allowing for the fact that two or more registers may share other functional factors.

In total, a set of six functional factors is needed to account for all of these registers (table 6.1). Of these, three are of a categorical nature:

1. Distinction among handicap, economy, and social distancing
2. Availability of a preexisting source
3. Availability of interlocutor feedback

Table 6.1 Matrix of conditioning factors of simple registers

	Categorical factors				Relative factors	
Register	Economy, Handicap, Social distancing	Preexisting source	Interlocutor feedback	Text constraints	Topic breadth	Participant status
Classified ads register	Economy	No	No	Planned	Broad	Equal
Headlinese	Economy	No	No	Planned	Broad	Unequal
Baby talk	Handicap	No	Yes	Unplanned	Narrow	Unequal
Foreigner talk	Handicap	No	Yes	Unplanned	Broad	Unequal
Avoidance registers	Social distancing	No	Yes	Unplanned	Narrow	Unequal
Pidgins	Handicap	No	Yes	Unplanned	Broad	Equal
Sports announcer talk	Economy	No	No	Unplanned	Narrow	Equal
Note-taking	Economy	Yes	No	Unplanned	Broad	Equal
Limericks	Economy	No	No	Planned	Narrow	Equal
Judges' clarifications	Handicap	Yes	Yes	Unplanned	Narrow	Unequal
Didactic texts	Handicap	Yes	No	Planned	Broad	Unequal

Three more are essentially relative, or continuously distributed:

4. Constraints on planning
5. Breadth of topic
6. Participant status

Seen from this multifactor perspective, the operation of each functional factor in each register must be analyzed in relation to the full set. For example, there is no guarantee that simplification from a preexisting source or the hypothesized operation of an innate sense of what constitutes linguistic simplicity alone will automatically produce similar texts since each resulting text type may have been shaped simultaneously by other factors. Similarly, although planning time is typically a function of a spoken versus a written dimension, academic note-taking (NT) shows that the parameter of economy can override that of opportunity for planning since spoken input must be converted into written form at a speed unsuited for that medium.[1] Similarly, judges' clarifications most probably follow well-rehearsed patterns, and planning time is reduced by the face-to-face nature of the interaction and the unpredictability of responses.

A second functional factor, availability of feedback, is normally a major characteristic of spoken registers. It offers speakers a chance to tailor their production to the capabilities of their interlocutor and, if necessary, to make both form and message more accessible in the light of an immediate response. Yet in sports announcer talk (SAT), it is the requirement for economy, not the availability of feedback, that is the key factor. In addition, some simple registers can operate in a displaced capacity across a wider field, as in the use of baby talk (BT) to address a pet, a lover, or even a plant (Hatch, 1983a; Ferguson, 1985). While in all three of these uses topics are likely to be narrowly focused, the handicap constraint, presumably, only applies to BT. Similarly both foreigner talk (FT) and pidgins can be used to mark social distance or to poke fun at a substrate group, a practice that usually relies on heavily conventionalized notions of language use (Meisel, 1977; Klein, 1986) in both the spoken and literary varieties of these registers (Mühlhaüsler, 1986; Larsen-Freeman & Long, 1991).

Another key element in this model is the role of the notion of participant status and its potential effect on interactional involvement.[2] Of course NT is a case apart since writers and readers are normally the same person. But in general, it should not be assumed that simple registers are too narrowly constrained to respond to interactional factors. As Bell writes, "at all levels of language variability, people are responding primarily to other people. Speakers are designing their style for their audience" (1984, p. 197). Similarly, Tannen observes that all language use "grows out of the conflicting human needs to be connected to other people and to be distant from them—that is, not to be engulfed by closeness" (1985, p. 125). Similarly, Ochs & Schieffelin stress that linguistic form cannot help being responsive to the fundamental need of language users to convey and assess moods and attitudes and that "almost any aspect of the linguistic system that is variable is a candidate for expressing affect" (1989, p. 22). Thus the operation of even the most primitive pidginized interaction must surely take affective considerations into account in the rapid computation of the multiplicity of functional factors.

Another advantage of this account of simple registers is that it allows the incorporation into the model of seemingly marginal registers. While avoidance registers, for example, might be marginalized because they cannot be accommodated on the basic handicap versus economy dimension, they can now be seen to differ from a more familiar variety such as BT in terms of only one factor. This is not to suggest that this alone makes an avoidance register a closer relative of BT than of, say, FT. The operation of a number of common functional factors may be nothing more than a coincidental surface manifestation of substantially different motivations. Yet the degree of commonality between these two registers shows that they conform broadly to a major prototype in which lack of planning time—among other factors—carries particular weight. Similarly, CAR and headlinese are closely associated with another prototype shaped essentially by the need for economy, unavailability of a source, and absence of feedback.

A further benefit of this attempt to relate the many facets of linguistic simplicity to one another is that it helps resolve some of the difficulties created by unsuitable terminology. Except in cases of deliberate obfuscation, the intention of the rational and cooperative language user posited by a Gricean perspective must be to maximize but not overdo clarity (Grice, 1975; Cooper, 1982). Thus, within the bounds deemed by each culture to divide appropriateness from hermeticism or prolixity, concepts may be clarified by a judge for a defendant's benefit or by a native speaker for a second language user. Traders clarify transactions for buyers from other linguistic communities, and headline writers know that their communicative intent will be best served if they reveal only so much but not too little. Caregivers clarify their affection toward infants, and apartment vendors specify the contents and attractions of their property for maximum effect. Thus as I argued, all successful communication rests at least in part on language that is maximally appropriate to a combination of communicative purpose and functional parameters. However, given the degree of variation in the functional parameters of each variety, the strategies available for each purpose will be as varied as the circumstances that condition them. As a result, a view of linguistic simplicity that reduces the concept to a matter of clarity and manageability may be an accurate reflection of language in use. But it is so general that it loses all explanatory power.

To be sure, any given terminology must mirror the values and metaphors of its parent culture. A particularly pertinent example is the conventional label *simplified register* itself, with its suggestion of top-down processing—that is, deletion from more elaborated underlying forms. This contrasts with the much more neutral label *simple register,* used throughout this book, which describes the register without making any claims about its origins or underlying mechanisms. Most probably, no single term can cover the multiplicity of functional factors that combine to shape the form of even some major types of simple registers. A less ambitious and ultimately more illuminating approach should be to identify the single most characteristic functional factor behind each register under study and to use that factor as an overall label. For example, since the need for economy is a major factor in the production of both CAR and NT, both of these varieties can be justifiably discussed under the label of economy register. Discussions of BT or FT would stress their handicap nature. Other registers would be conceptualized as essentially planned discourse of an economy type (such as limericks) or of an economy, spoken, and noninteractive variety (such as SAT). Thus the approach succeeds where all-encompassing definitions fail in that it provides an infinitely adaptable mapping of form to ever-evolving situations.

Processing

Innateness

I have shown that despite a substantial degree of cross-category variation in the frequency of function words, CAR is characterized by minimal syntactic elaboration as measured by the relative rarity of function words. I have also presented evidence that, to the extent that function words appear in CAR texts, their presence may in some cases be due to the collocational rigidity of the lexicogrammatical contexts in which they appear. In this, CAR confirms the observation, most clearly articulated by Ferguson (1982), that simple registers share a substantial number of common features (see appendix A for full details of these features). If we are to follow Ferguson in positing a possibly innate human ability to dispense with unnecessarily elaborated form whenever appropriate, evidence from CAR can certainly be interpreted as supporting this hypothesis.

If valid, the notion of a possible universal dimension to linguistic simplicity may, as Ferguson (1982) argues, have far-reaching implications for syntactic theory, psycholinguistics, and sociolinguistics, and further cross-linguistic evidence in this area must ultimately illuminate our understanding of human language. But as Ferguson himself acknowledges, features common to a number of simple registers "may have different origins, fulfill different functions, and serve simultaneously as parts of other systems" (1983, p. 168). To be sure, an innateness hypothesis captures part of the process, but as I have shown, the nature of linguistic simplicity cannot be reduced to the dispensability of function words and morphological markers, however cross-linguistically validated this may be. In any case, Fathman's (1977) criticism that this cross-linguistic validation rested on a relatively narrow empirical base remains true today since the empirical basis for theoretical assessments of linguistic simplicity has not grown substantially in recent years, despite the occasional appearance of studies of specific registers such as the one I present in this book.

A further weakness of the innateness hypothesis is that it presupposes a view of simple discourse as the product of reduction from more elaborated forms, with deletion playing a major part (see, for example, Ferguson, 1975, 1982). Central to this analysis is the traditional notion that *telegraphic* (Gunter, 1963) or *elliptical* (Matthews, 1981) deletion affects more elaborated underlying sentences by removing, top-down as it were, elements made superfluous by constraints of the handicap or economy type.[3] However, this study has shown that CAR texts often bear very little relation to any recognizable form of the kind normally deemed to represent an underlying grammar. With expansion to a more elaborated form ultimately depending on pragmatic or contextual clues, informants are rarely in agreement on what the underlying structure of CAR texts might have consisted of.

This does not in itself constitute evidence that an underlying structure did not exist and that deletion plays little or no part in achieving linguistic simplicity. Yet the suggestion that the minimally elaborated form of, say, an auto ad is primarily the product of deletion processes implies that ad writers must go about the production of their texts in a singularly inefficient manner, especially since other—and possibly simultaneous—strategies may be available. In contrast to assumptions of a top-down strategy as the only—or even the major—route available to language users in the production of CAR texts and of simple language in general, a bottom-up view argues that language users may not cut back from underlying forms toward a common core, or set of linguistic features shared by all simple registers. Instead, the core itself is seen as the default under which all language users normally operate unless they choose—or are led by functional factors—to elaborate on it in order to operate more successfully in a more appropriate, more elaborated register. Thus the alleged ungrammaticality of many simple texts is not the—to the grammarian, unfortunate—byproduct of deletion processes but rather the point of departure for maximally appropriate linguistic elaboration.

The idea that the problem may have been viewed upside down can be traced to Corder (1977) and Ochs (1979). Both suggest that elaborated forms are not standard, but in fact complex, and that much of language use, as well as language learning, consists of degrees of elaboration of basic forms. Chafe also questions the assumption of a "top-down application of a branching tree structure" (1987, p. 44). Instead, he stresses the importance for language users of being aware of what is appropriate at each stage of production. Since a theory of linguistic simplicity must ultimately explain how fully competent speakers come to produce so much language that falls outside the predictions of the literary grammar, a bottom-up approach is at least as helpful as assumptions of top-down processing. In addition, a bottom-up approach is fully compatible with the view that innate mechanisms may play a part in the production of this and other simple registers. Perhaps, when faced with constraints of the handicap or economy type, language users instinctively rely in part on strategies characteristic of earlier stages in their linguistic development. Rather than being gradually replaced as the learner progresses, these strategies may be retained, "to be relied upon under certain communicative conditions" (Ochs, 1979, p. 52). Language users may thus have the capacity to erect upon the common core a linguistic edifice whose degree of elaboration reflects cognitive, functional, and social conditions.

Conventionalization

In chapter 4, I have highlighted the extensive role played by prefabricated segments in the linguistic structure of CAR. In addition, I have just argued that top-down explanations for linguistic simplicity are not as axiomatic as has been assumed and that the production of maximally appropriate language may be instead a matter of elaborating over a basic core. Thus a model of production of simple registers needs to allow for the insertion into texts of conventionalized, prefabricated sequences as part of this process of elaboration. Following Sinclair (1987), I am tempted to go further and to surmise that the language user's first assumption is that language is primarily made up of familiar collocations and idiomlike strings, and that most messages are interpretable by this principle. Most probably, familiar collocations are linked in long-term memory with the familiar concepts and speech acts that they normally serve to encode, along with a degree of pragmatic and stylistic information that narrows the choice of best fit for each stored segment (Levelt, 1989). Frequently heard or used configurations may be stored as wholes—despite the redundancy involved—while novel or rarely needed patterns and collocations may be assembled piece by piece along generative lines when the need arises (de Beaugrande & Dressler, 1981; Ferguson, 1983; Peters, 1983).

Since language production—among other operations of the human mind—is typically constrained not by lack of storage capacity but by retrieval and reassembly difficulties, the role played by stored collocations is to free users from the need to reinvent preexisting forms, enabling them to attend to matters of greater pragmatic and interactional consequence. Thus as Tannen (1987) argues, what constitutes the grammar of a variety may be less a system of abstract rules than a multitude of actual pieces of discourse remembered from earlier events, retrieved and reshaped to the requirements of each subsequent context. Perhaps it is this accumulation of previously encountered discourse that constitutes the deep structure of the system, and it is the ability to retrieve elements from this partially abstracted store that constitutes competence. Most natural language is thus produced with the help of what Pawley & Syder call a "phrase book with grammatical notes" (1983b, p. 220), occupying a theoretical position somewhere between syntactic rules and the lexicon. In language use, the extent to which syntactic rules will be invoked to link prefabricated segments will depend on the interplay of the kind of functional factors that I have built into my multifunctional model of linguistic simplicity. In CAR, the influence of spatial constraints will be one—but only one—of these functional factors.

Integrating innateness and conventionalization

An integrated view of the nature of CAR thus argues that the register reflects the interplay of additional and simultaneous processes. A major part of constructing a CAR text consists of incorporating prefabricated and prepatterned segments at varying levels of syntactic elaboration. To the extent that the need for explicitness and a desire to index interactional involvement require, the degree of elaboration is increased, occasionally to the point of meeting the requirements of the literary grammar in full. But given the stringent spatial constraints of the register, there is a simultaneous incentive for the writer to stay relatively close to a range of—possibly innate—core strategies and to leave out of the elaboration process dispensable features of English such as articles, auxiliaries, and copulas.

To the extent that CAR relies on an interplay between these two processes—the incorporation of prefabricated elements plus a sense of what is dispensable in syntactic structure—some parallels with language acquisition are worth noting. Over the past two decades, research has comprehensively documented the tendency among children and second-language learners to base a great deal of their initial language acquisition on chunks that are extensively practiced before they appear to be analyzed (see, for example, Hakuta, 1974; Krashen & Scarcella, 1978; Peters, 1983; Snow, 1986). In addition, the transition by children from largely formulaic to increasingly creative, rule-governed language production is marked by the presence of obligatory morphemes in the former and their simultaneous absence in the latter (Miecznikowski & Andersen, 1986), a combination reminiscent of the language of CAR. While these phenomena do not constitute direct evidence for the role of prefabricated segments in simple registers, they show that these segments were once relevant to all language users. This process of transition from initial ad hoc strategies to increasing elaboration of the structure of discourse recalls Givón's (1979) contention that children may not acquire syntax in a Chomskyan sense but rather a communicative system of a much more rudimentary sort, which may only later be modified, that is, elaborated to satisfy the requirements of the dominant adult grammar. Thus the diachronic development of languages and the synchronic, on-line production of maximally appropriate discourse under a variety of functional parameters may parallel each other in a manner to which the term *panchronic* is well suited (Heine, Claudi, & Hünnemeyer, 1991, p. 258).

Linguistic simplicity and grammatical theory

If prefabricated segments indeed play a part in the construction of linguistic form, then communicative competence must consist at least in part of the ability to move swiftly from one segment to the next (Sinclair, 1988; Kjellmer, 1991). This is as true of CAR and other simple registers as it is of linguistic production in general. To be sure, humans are theoretically endowed with the potential to produce and understand an unlimited number of sentences, provided these are sanctioned by the dominant grammar of their language. However, acknowledging this axiom does not constitute evidence that language users make use of this ability to the extent assumed in Chomskyan linguistics. On the contrary, the study of a narrow register such as CAR shows that the Chomskyan claim, exemplified by Kaye, that "in our day-to-day world, most of what we hear and speak is novel" (1989, p. 2) needs to be tested in context.

This adds credence to the view that retention of the sentences of the literary grammar as the basic units of linguistic analysis is not appropriate in all contexts. Indeed, doubts about the suitability of the sentence as the central focus of linguistic analysis have been expressed by commentators as varied as Pawley & Syder (1983b), Chafe (1985), Milroy & Milroy (1985), and Hopper (1988), among others. This runs contrary to the generativist assumption (Chomsky, 1965) that sentences represent the expression of the system held mentally by an ideal speaker-hearer, representative of a homogeneous speech community. This is a view that sees grammar as an a priori set of rules which precedes discourse, a static construct, fully present at all times in the mind of the speaker, and fully detachable from discourse (Hopper, 1988).

Register variation does not easily fit into such tidy notions of linguistic competence, and a generative framework is not likely to be helpful in accounting for the variability that is inherent in language use, given that the approach is explicit in its determination to divorce language from its social context (Milroy & Milroy, 1985; Cheshire, 1987). Thus it would be misguided to try to reconcile the structure of simple registers with the rules induced by generative linguists from the sentences that serve as their data. Instead, it should be remembered that even in a spatially constrained register such as CAR, variation in the degree of syntactic elaboration of texts correlates with variation in functional factors. Thus it is to these functional factors, not to a body of made-up, decontextualized sentences, that simple texts need to be related.

Indeed, far from being ill formed in relation to the sentences of the literary grammar, simple registers exhibit a degree of internal consistency that reveals the systematic influence of functional factors and which makes these registers, at least in part, independent of the literary grammar. After all, like every other register, the formal written discourse on which the rules of the literary grammar are based is the way it is in response to a specific set of functional factors. Once that discourse comes under the influence of a different set of factors, it acquires a set of features that distinguishes it from neighboring types. As a result, registers are not more or less grammatical. Rather, they are more or less like one another in that they exhibit degrees of syntactic elaboration which can be related not to some absolute standard but to the set of functional parameters that constrains the production of each utterance. As Nair writes of the language of classified ads, "it is the utterance, bounded by speaker-to-hearer reciprocal relationships, and emphatically not the sentence ... that motivates enquiry in these areas of linguistic investigation" (1992, p. 229). If adult communicative competence includes the ability, both receptively and productively, to match each familiar register to its functional correlates, it is insufficient for linguistic inquiry to limit itself to the explication of the individual's mental organization. How register variation "is shared and conventionalized, how it is transmitted and acquired, and how it changes through time" is just as central to linguistic inquiry as explications of the phonological, syntactic, and semantic properties of linguistic systems (Ferguson, 1983, p. 154).

Far from dismissing register variation as an irrelevant—or, at best, an inconvenient—distraction, a theory that sees language use as shaped by the encoder's ongoing assessment of functional parameters gives language variation a central role not only at the empirical stage in linguistic analysis but also in discussions of the nature of grammar. Functional variation must be interpreted "not just as variation in the use of language, but rather as something that is built in, as the very foundation, to the organization of language itself" (Halliday & Hasan, 1989, p. 17). The functional dimension, therefore, is not simply the use to which linguistic form is put once it has been shaped in the mind through the application of abstract rules. It is also a fundamental property of language itself, playing a key part both in the synchronic construction of linguistic form and in the diachronic evolution of language.

A further implication of the integration of register variation into grammatical models is that the approach makes frequency of occurrence a central element in linguistic analysis. As Uspensky & Zhivov (1977) argue, linguists confronted with violations of the principles they postulate tend to explain variation as largely random and to pass over systematic violations of the grammar they postulate. In generative linguistics, the exception—if deemed grammatical—calls for a revision of whatever rule it may break. From a probabilistic point of view, however, "the exception is allowed to bear such weight as its frequency of occurrence requires," and grammar can rightly "treat of what is almost always, or usually, or not often, or only seldom the case" (Burrows, 1992, p. 172). Moreover, each instance has the power to redefine the system since each observation either maintains its present state or shifts its probabilities in one direction or the other. Thus it is "the transformation of instance into system" (Halliday, 1991, p. 34), observable only through recourse to corpus-based techniques, that allows the observer to accumulate instances, relate them to functional factors, build up a synchronic picture of the system—in other words, write a grammar—and ultimately monitor diachronic variations in patterns of frequency.

Suggestions for further research

Given the relative rarity of accounts of simple registers, further research in this field must first aim for greater descriptive validity. In general, this means adding to the current body of studies of simple registers, such as the language of telephone messages. With reference to CAR, it involves reexamining current perceptions of linguistic simplicity cross-linguistically, as pioneered by van Dijk (1988) in his work on headlines in Arabic and Japanese, but framed within a methodology capable of handling a large corpus, such as Biber's (1988, 1994). This type of work should take as its material a corpus of classified ads from comparable ad categories published in languages that are substantially different from English—Japanese, Chinese, Finnish, or Turkish, for example.[4] Cross-linguistic research should also examine the occurrence in simple registers of prefabricated segments and the role that these segments may play in providing the building blocks of simple texts.

A second avenue for further research is the development of conventionalization in CAR. While the role of conventions in language use is widely recognized, little is known about the rate of development of the major conventions of this register from inception to generalized acceptance (Ferguson, 1994). Given that ad writers readily admit to referring for editorial guidance to the newspaper in which their text is to appear, it would be revealing to examine the appearance, spread, and solidification of discoursal conventions in a still emerging text type such as personal ads, for example. Possible candidates for study include the spread of specific register markers in personal ads or some shifting in the conventions regulating the sequencing of information across a range of ad categories. Another, following Nair (1992), is the search for some of the dominant social ideologies that may—overtly or covertly—help shape the register and give its form part of its resilience.

Finally, further research should continue to explore the issue of writers' personal motivations for elaborating the language of their texts. Although I have shown that the degree of syntactic elaboration can be linked to a requirement for explicitness and to expectations of interactional involvement, it does not follow that other functional factors are not relevant and do not need to be uncovered. I have shown that even the need for greater explicitness and the closer interpersonal interaction predicted by the circumstances of job and personal ad writers correlates with a frequency of function words that is still markedly lower than that across a broad range of registers. Research might, for example, consider the possibility that those CAR writers who elaborate most are responding to more than the operation of functional factors on discrete function words. Clearly, a key role of the finer details of language is that they serve to carry interactionally essential information such as the participant's status (Hudson, 1980). Thus a move in the direction of greater syntactic elaboration may be related to an association between minimal elaboration and socially denigrated varieties such as BT or FT. Perhaps CAR writers are aware that, in the reader's mind, maturity, authoritativeness, and sophistication are not likely to be associated with limited vocabulary and bare-bone syntax—in short, with infantlike language. Since writing a classified ad is an attempt to advance the writer's interests through language, success—that is, being selected over the claims of competitors—critically depends on highlighting one's appeal. If so, it may be crucial to bring to bear on the composition process any strategy that offers a chance of making that all-important positive impression. The ability to weave appropriately elaborated linguistic form around meaning may be an essential part of functioning successfully as a language user.

APPENDIX A: SUMMARY OF FEATURES OF LINGUISTIC SIMPLIFICATION

A	B
More complex or unsimplified linguistic structure, as source or target	Simpler or simplified linguistic structure

Lexicon

Larger vocabulary in a given semantic area or overall	Smaller vocabulary; generic terms rather than specific
Compounds and morphologically complex words	Monomorphemic words; paraphrases of complex words

Syntax

Sentences with subordinate clauses	No subordinate clauses; parataxis
Variable word order conditioned by syntax (e.g.: inversions, negative placement)	Invariant word order
Presence of copulas, pronouns, function words	Absence of copulas, pronouns, function words

Morphology

Extensive inflectional systems	No inflections
Allomorphy of stems	Invariant stems (e.g., full forms as opposed to contractions)

Phonology

Consonant clusters	CV [consonant-vowel] monosyllables and CVCV [consonant-vowel-consonant-vowel] disyllables
Polysyllabic words	

From Charles A. Ferguson, Simplified registers and linguistic theory, in *Exceptional language and linguistics*, Lorraine K. Obler & Lise Menn, eds. (New York: Academic Press, 1982), p. 60.

APPENDIX B: CORPUS SELECTION CRITERIA

Recycler

Autos: Ten ads per year of manufacture between 1981 and 1990, with every tenth ad selected to ensure variety of make and price, beginning alternately from beginning and end of consecutive years for better coverage of the alphabetical range, to a maximum of six lines.

Personals: Every other ad, 50 from the *Females Seeking Males* section and 50 from the *Males Seeking Females* section, excluding all ads beginning with bold, capitalized headings, which are usually substantially longer than the standard four lines.

Apartments: Every tenth ad, excluding those with bold, capitalized headings, which are usually substantially longer than a self-imposed limit of five lines.

Jobs: Every other ad, except those with bold, capitalized headings, which are usually substantially longer than a self-imposed limit of five lines. All categories appearing under separate subheadings in the newspaper were merged in the CAR corpus, e.g., sales, office, delivery, child care.

LA Weekly

Autos: All ads for cars manufactured between 1981 and 1990, excluding those in boxes with capitalized headings, to a maximum of six lines.

Appendix B: Corpus Selection Criteria

Personals: Every sixth ad, beginning from the end of *Women Seeking Men* and *Men Seeking Women* sections to avoid overabundance of ads beginning with the letter *A*, up to a maximum of six lines.

Apartments: Every ad up to six lines, excluding usually longer, boxed ads.

Jobs: Every ad, excluding usually longer, boxed ads, up to a maximum of six lines.

APPENDIX C: GLOSSARY OF ABBREVIATIONS

This glossary includes all abbreviations in ads cited in this book together with their most likely interpretations. Lowercase and uppercase variants of the same type are listed only once, in lower case (such as *BR* and *br*, both entered as *br*), as are entries that differ only in punctuation (such as *a/c* and *a.c.*, entered as *ac*).

ac	air conditioned	beaut	beautiful
ad	advertising	BH	Beverly Hills
adj	adjacent	Bill W	Bill Wilson
adjac	adjacent		(founder of Alcoholics
adjc	adjacent		Anonymous)
aft	after	bldg	building
agt	agent	blk	black
air	air conditioned	blk	block
alum	aluminum	blt-ins	built-ins
appl	appliances	Blvd	boulevard
apprec	appreciate	bod	body
apt	apartment	br	bedroom
apts	apartments	brks	brakes
auto	automatic	brn	brown
avail	available	brs	bedrooms
ba	bathroom	bus	business
batt	battery	c&d	carpet and drapes
BBQ	barbecue	CA	California
bckgrnd	background	carb	carburetor
bd	bedroom	cass	cassette
bdrm	bedroom	ceil	ceiling
bdrms	bedrooms	cln	clean

Appendix C: Glossary of Abbreviations

clr	clear	grg	garage
co	company	grn	green
comm	commission	grt	great
comml	communal	hb	hatchback
comp	compensation	hi	high
cond	condition	hp	horsepower
crpt	carpet	hr	hour
cyl	cylinders	hrs	hours
dep	deposit	immed	immediately
DHF	divorced Hispanic female	incl	included
		int	interior
dist	distribute	k	n,000 dollars
DJM	divorced Jewish male	k	n,000 miles
dng	dining	kitch	kitchen
dr	door	LA	Los Angeles
drs	doors	lic	license
dshwshr	dishwasher	limo	limousine
DWF	divorced white female	lk	like
DWM	divorced white male	lndry	laundry
ea	each	loc	location
eng	engine	lrg	large
eve	evening	LSASE	large, self-addressed envelope
eves	evenings		
exec	executive	lt	light
exp	experience	lvg	living
ext	exterior		
F	female	m	n,000 miles
fac	facilities	mi	n,000 miles
facils	facilities	micro	microwave
fplc	fireplace	min	minimum
Fri	Friday	mo	month
frplc	fireplace	Mon	Monday
ft	feet	mtr	motor
ft	full time	mvg	moving
gd	good	N	north
gen	generous	natl	national

Appendix C: Glossary of Abbreviations

nd	need	SAF	single Asian female
nd	no drugs	SAM	single Asian male
ndd	needed	Sat	Saturday
nds	needs	SBF	single black female
nr	near		
ns	nonsmoking	SBM	single black male
NYC	New York City		
obo	or best offer	sec	secure
		sec	security
p	power	secy	secretary
parkg	parking	sep	separate
pb	power brakes	sero-pos	sero-positive
pckg	package	SF	single female
pd	paid	sgls	singles
pic	picture	SHF	single Hispanic female
pls	please		
pnt	paint	SJF	single Jewish female
PO	post office	SJM	single Jewish male
PR	public relations	sks	seeks
pref	preferred	sm	small
prkng	parking	SM	single male
ps	power steering	snrf	sunroof
pt	part time	spac	spacious
pvt	private	spcl	special
pw	power windows	spd	speed
r&s	refrigerator and stove	sq	square
		St	street
RE	real estate	ster	stereo
refrig	refrigerator	stv	stove
refs	references	SW	single woman
reg	regular	SWF	single white female
rep	representative	SWM	single white male
reqd	required	TBA	to be announced
rm	room	tel	telephone
rpr	repair	Thurs	Thursday
S	single	trans	transmission
S	south	transp	transportation
s&r	stove and refrigerator	trd	trade

Appendix C: Glossary of Abbreviations

UCLA	University of California at Los Angeles	wknds	weekends
		WLA	West Los Angeles
		WM	white male
uphols	upholstery	wpm	words per minute
vy	very	wtd	wanted
w	with	x	extension
w&d	washer and dryer	xlnt	excellent
		xtra	extra
Wed	Wednesday		
WF	white female	yo	years old
wgn	wagon	yr	year
wht	white	yrs	years

APPENDIX D: TEST OF EDITORIAL INTERFERENCE IN *RECYCLER* ADS

Texts were written with actual items of personal property in mind, realistically described and priced. All texts were scripted in advance, with no abbreviations, but with the sequencing of segments such as color and price deliberately varied. The texts were telephoned on four separate dates (January 17, 18, 19, and 20, 1993). They were accepted by four different operators, who were asked to identify themselves. None suggested any editorial alterations whatsoever. Conversations held on January 25, 1993, with classified advertising editors for both the *Recycler* and the *LA Weekly* confirmed that the practice conformed to guidelines given to operators receiving ads over the telephone. Editorial standardization was immediately apparent only in the case of the telephone number, which was dictated once and then automatically added at the end of each ad. Texts were dictated as follows, to appear under the following headings:

Dining room furniture

Table, jet black surface and uprights, very sturdy and stylish, $75 obo, 310-397-1234

Bedroom furniture

Chest of drawers, matching pair, off white, three drawers each, very clean, $85 the pair, 310-397-1234

Appendix D: Test of Editorial Interference in Recycler Ads

Living room furniture

Armchairs, one swivel and reclining, one fixed, $85 each obo, both stylish, comfortable, excellent condition, 310-397-1234

Miscellaneous furniture

Bookcase, $50 obo, five shelves, excellent condition, jet black wood, 310-397-1234

The ads were printed in the Los Angeles edition of the *Recycler* dated January 21–28, 1993. They appeared as follows:

> TABLE, jet black surface & uprights, vy sturdy & stylish, $75 obo 310-397-1234
>
> CHEST of drawers, matching pair, off wht, 3 drawers ea, vy cln, $85 pr 310-397-1234
>
> ARMCHAIRS, 1 swivel & reclining, 1 fixed, $85 ea obo, both stylish, comf, xlnt cond 310-397-1234
>
> BOOKCASE, $50 obo, 5 shelves, xlnt cond, jet black wood 310-397-1234

NOTES

Chapter 1

1. An early example of the influence of the generative paradigm is Ferguson's (1975) pioneering experiment in which subjects were asked to offer "foreigner talk" (FT) versions of well-formed sentences.

2. Although linguists working within the generative paradigm do not take the degree of formality into consideration when providing intuitional data to back up their theories, there is a sense—noted by analysts such as Milroy & Milroy (1985) and Cheshire (1987), among others—that these data come much closer to formal, typically written language than to informal, typically spoken registers.

3. Among more recent labels describing baby talk (BT) are *caretaker speech*, *motherese*, and Snow's (1986) *child-directed speech*. However, the fact that the term *BT* is solidly established justifies its continued use here.

4. When questioned informally, many classified ad writers report looking at recent ads before imitating what they see as an appropriate style for a given publication. Although this constitutes little more than anecdotal evidence for the process of conventionalization in language, it may constitute a rich source of information for future research.

5. Given my chosen definition of what constitutes a register, this a priori identification of CAR as a register should predict that its linguistic form will correlate closely with circumstances of use for the register as a whole. That is, all classified ads should exhibit largely similar linguistic form. In practice, as I will show, variation in topic and function within the register—as in auto versus personal ads—is mirrored by variation in linguistic form across these two (and other) ad categories. However, since a line must be drawn somewhere, I continue to regard the language of classified ads as a whole as a single register despite systematic internal variation within it, and I analyze this variation under the subheadings of *ad categories*, which might just as plausibly be labeled *subregisters*.

Chapter 2

1. Given the spread of negative advertising in TV advertising in the United States, it may now be more appropriate to make the opposite assumption—namely, that anything in the content of a commercial will be unfavorable to the rival product that is negatively featured.

2. For a trenchant rebuttal of Sperber & Wilson's (1986) relevance theory, see Levinson (1989).

3. Dates of publication are November 7, 1991, for the *Recycler*; November 29, 1991, and January 10 and January 31, 1992, for the *LA Weekly*.

4. As information concerning the circulation and readership of both the *LA Weekly* and the *Recycler* was not available in published form, it was obtained in telephone conversations with the respective editors on February 3, 1993.

5. Since word count facilities in most software—including the WordPerfect 5.1 originally used—count contractions as one word, all contractions marked by an apostrophe were separated manually before the word count (*I'm* becoming *I' m*, for example).

6. Original telephone and house numbers have been changed, but the actual number of digits has been respected. Original line breaks as well as original typographical features such as punctuation and spellings have been retained throughout. Some commas were used for what looked to be periods in the original but needed to be commas grammatically.

7. Personal ads also form the basis of at least one novel by a respected modern writer, Paul Theroux's *Chicago Loop*.

Chapter 3

1. For a full treatment of these and other views of quantitative approaches to the study of language variation, see Milroy (1987).

2. Both the *LOB* and *Brown* corpora contain texts published in 1961. The present study refers to word counts listed in the tagged versions of both corpora.

3. Throughout this book, salient passages within illustrations from the CAR corpus have been underscored for convenience.

4. Counts for tokens of individual features were made manually through the *Search* command in WordPerfect 5.1.

5. Modals analyzed here are *may, might, must, can, could, shall, should, will*, and *would*. Tokens of *won't* are listed in *Brown* but not in *LOB*, where they are assumed to have been counted under *will*.

6. Negatives analyzed here are limited to forms occurring in the corpus, namely, *no, not, n't, non-*, and *nor*.

7. Counts for the CAR and *LOB* corpora include *and, 'n*, and *&*. In contrast, no separate count of *&* is made in *Brown*.

Chapter 4

1. For a comprehensive survey of sources on conventionalization and a discussion of its implications, see Atkinson (1991).

2. Bartsch (1987) distinguishes between *conventions*, based on a mu-

tual, often tacit contract, and *norms*, which imply an element of coercion. Conventions may come to assume the force of norms as they pass beyond their originators, especially across generations. However, the distinction is more one of degree than of essence, and I do not pursue it in this book.

3. The *LA Weekly*'s editorial policy bars the use of abbreviations except in segments of the *SBM* type. The motive for this ban is unclear since ads are priced per word, not per line. This prohibition appears to be the exception rather than the rule in publications of this type.

4. Abbreviations excluded from this count include items with no elaborated form (e.g., *V6, GTX, OK*), items with a rarely used elaborated form (e.g., *lbs, am-fm, ft, Mr., am/pm*), items whose elaborated form would be inappropriate in this context (e.g., *1st, n'n*), and items with quasilexical status (e.g., *TV, VCR, JVC, condo, Mac, gym, CD, VW*).

5. Counts of word tokens and, once identified manually, of word types, were performed through the COUNT command in WordPerfect 5.1.

6. Because this corpus consists of unusually short texts, type-to-token ratios were calculated for each ad category as a whole rather than for each individual ad.

7. Frequency counts include all tokens of a form, written out or abbreviated, as in *building* and *bldng*.

8. It would be useful, as one reviewer suggests, to offer a comparison between frequency of frameworks in CAR and that in a wider corpus. However, the *LOB* corpus, on which I relied in the previous section for comparison of the role of lexical collocations in CAR and in wider usage, does not list structural collocations of the type examined here.

9. In this section, counts exclude a small number of abbreviations, such as *n/s*, for which both *no smoking/no smoker* and *nonsmoking/nonsmoker* are possible readings.

10. A prototypical example of this type of analysis is Nair's (1992) comparison of the ideological foundations of a corpus of Indian, British, and American personal (matrimonial) ads. Nair converts syntactic constituents into rewrite rules and tree diagrams and describes their semantic realization in Hallidayan terms such as *descriptor*. The approach is valid as long as texts unambiguously exhibit recognizable syntactic features. This is clearly true of Nair's corpus, in which levels of syntactic elaboration are relatively high, as it is to some extent of the job and personal ad categories of the CAR corpus. But the minimally elaborated texts of apartment and, especially, auto ads are largely antithetic to the very notion of constituent analysis and little would be gained from the high degree of speculation that would be required concerning possible underlying syntactic forms for these texts.

11. More generally, the pattern of information sequencing found in auto ads is also consistent with a tendency in English for multiple modifiers to

be sequenced in rough order of increasing subjectivity. That is, in *an expensive green car*, the modifying adjective closest to the head noun can be said to be the most objective and least controversial of the two. In other words, distance from the head noun increases with the subjectivity of the assessment being made.

Chapter 5

1. All entries in the tables in this chapter have been rounded up or down to a single decimal. Entries of 0.1 are equal to 0.1 or less.
2. To follow Hatch & Lazaraton (1991), a nonparametric Mann Whitney test is preferred to a *t* test because a normal distribution is not apparent in at least one of the ad categories.
3. It should not be assumed that the inclusion of one of the six features under study is the only major factor in creating a text of greater length. Some ads are longer than others for a variety of reasons, not least pricing policy. Yet the two phenomena cannot be entirely unrelated.
4. Comparison with *LOB* and *Brown* covers only those first and second pronouns occurring in the CAR corpus, namely, *I*, *me*, *my*, *mine*, *we*, *us*, *our*, *ours*, and *(let)'s* for first person, and *you*, *your*, *yours*, and *yourself* for second person.
5. See Biber (1988) for a comprehensive review of sources in this area.
6. Direct comparison is not entirely valid since I merge both functions of *be* as verb and auxiliary, whereas Biber (1988) focuses on *be* as main verb only.
7. As explained in chapter 4, figures for abbreviations apply only to *Recycler* ads because the *LA Weekly*'s editorial policy prohibits the use of abbreviations except for codes of the *SBM* type.

Chapter 6

1. This must also be true of the registers of telephone messages and personal diaries, although these have received little research attention so far.
2. Discussions of interactional *involvement* can be credited to Chafe (1980) and Tannen (1982a, 1982b). Givón (1979) writes along similar lines but chooses the term *bonding* instead. For their part, Eisenstein & Starbuck (1989) and He (1992) refer to *emotional investment* and *social alignment*, respectively.
3. This type of deletion contrasts with *contextual* (Gunter, 1963) or *contracted* (Matthews, 1981) deletion, in which a missing element can be recovered uniquely from a preceding clause or turn. This is a syntax-based strategy whose contribution to textual cohesion is unquestioned (see, for example, Halliday & Hasan, 1976).

4. Informal observation suggests that Japanese apartment ads rely almost exclusively on *kanji* (Chinese) characters, which combine maximum semantic content and spatial savings. This contrasts with a current trend among younger Japanese writers to move away from *kanji* in favor of the more modern-looking—but spatially much less economical—*katakana* syllabary. Most important, morphosyntactic markers—which normally follow *kanji* content words and are written in the *hiragana* syllabary—appear to have been dispensed with altogether in classified ads.

REFERENCES

Aarts, Jan. (1991). Intuition-based and observation-based grammars. In Aijmer, Karin, & Altenberg, Bengt (eds.), *English corpus linguistics* (pp. 44–62). London: Longman.
Aitchison, Jean. (1987). Reproductive furniture and extinguished professors. In Steele, Ross & Threadgold, Terry (eds.), *Language topics: Essays in honour of Michael Halliday* (vol. 2, pp. 3–14). Amsterdam: John Benjamins.
Atkinson, Dwight. (1991). Discourse analysis and written discourse conventions. In Kaplan, Robert B., et al. (eds.), *Annual review of applied linguistics* (vol. 11, pp. 57–76). New York: Cambridge University Press.
Atkinson, Dwight, & Biber, Douglas. (1994). Register: A review of empirical research. In Biber, Douglas, & Finegan, Edward (eds.), *Sociolinguistic perspectives on register* (pp. 351–385). New York: Oxford University Press.
Ayres, Joe. (1992). Personal ads: An exploratory investigation into the relationships among ad characteristics, communication apprehension, and contact. *Communication Reports*, 5:67–72.
Baring-Gould, William S. (1967). *The lure of the limerick: An uninhibited history.* New York: Clarkson Potter.
Bartsch, Renate. (1987). *Norms of language: Theoretical and practical aspects.* London: Longman.
Beaman, Karen. (1984). Coordination and subordination revisited: Syntactic complexity in spoken and written narrative discourse. In Tannen, Deborah (ed.), *Coherence in spoken and written discourse* (pp. 45–80). Norwood, N.J.: Ablex.
Bell, Allan. (1984). Language style as audience design. *Language in Society*, 13: 145–204.
Bell, Allan. (1991). *The language of news media.* Oxford: Blackwell.
Benson, Morton, Benson, Evelyn, & Ilson, Robert. (1986). *The BBI combinatory dictionary of English: A guide to word combinations.* Amsterdam: John Benjamins.
Besnier, Niko. (1986). Register as a sociolinguistic unit: Defining formality. In Connor-Linton, Jeff, Hall, Christopher J., & McGinnis, Mary (eds.), *Social and cognitive perspectives on language* (pp. 25–63).

Southern California Occasional Papers in Linguistics, vol. 11. Los Angeles: University of Southern California.

Bhatia, Vijay K. (1993). *Analysing genre: Language use in professional settings.* London: Longman.

Biber, Douglas. (1988). *Variation across speech and writing.* Cambridge: Cambridge University Press.

Biber, Douglas. (1992). On the complexity of discourse complexity. *Discourse Processes, 15*: 133–163.

Biber, Douglas. (1994). An analytical framework for register studies. In Biber, Douglas, & Finegan, Edward (eds.), *Sociolinguistic perspectives on register* (pp. 31–56). New York: Oxford University Press.

Bruthiaux, Paul. (1993). Linguistic simplicity and the language of classified ads. Unpublished Ph.D. dissertation, University of Southern California, Los Angeles.

Bruthiaux, Paul. (1994). Me Tarzan, You Jane: Linguistic simplification in "Personal Ads" register. In Biber, Douglas, & Finegan, Edward (eds.), *Sociolinguistic perspectives on register* (pp. 136–154). New York: Oxford University Press.

Burrows, John F. (1992). Computers and the study of literature. In Butler, Christopher S. (ed.), *Computers and written texts* (pp. 167–204). Oxford: Blackwell.

Cervantes, Raoul, & Gainer, Glenn. (1992). The effects of syntactic simplification and repetition on listening comprehension. *TESOL Quarterly, 26*: 767–770.

Chafe, Wallace L. (1980). The deployment of consciousness in the production of a narrative. In Chafe, Wallace L. (ed.), *The pear stories: Cognitive, cultural, and linguistic aspects of narrative production* (pp. 9–50). Norwood, N.J.: Ablex.

Chafe, Wallace L. (1982). Integration and involvement in speaking, writing, and oral literature. In Tannen, Deborah (ed.), *Spoken and written language: Exploring orality and literacy* (pp. 35–53). Norwood, N.J.: Ablex.

Chafe, Wallace L. (1985). Linguistic differences produced by differences between speaking and writing. In Olson, David R., Torrance, Nancy, & Hildyard, Angela (eds.), *Literacy, language and learning: The nature and consequences of reading and writing* (pp. 105–123). Cambridge: Cambridge University Press.

Chafe, Wallace L. (1986). Writing in the perspective of speaking. In Cooper, Charles R., & Greenbaum, Sidney (eds.), *Studying writing: Linguistic approaches* (pp. 12–39). Beverly Hills, Cal.: Sage.

Chafe, Wallace L. (1987). Cognitive constraints on information flow. In Tomlin, Russell S. (ed.), *Coherence and grounding in discourse* (pp. 21–51). Amsterdam: John Benjamins.

Cheshire, Jenny. (1987). Syntactic variation, the linguistic variable, and sociolinguistic theory. *Linguistics, 25*: 257–282.

Chiat, Shulamuth. (1986). Personal pronouns. In Fletcher, Paul, & Garman, Michael (eds.), *Language acquisition: Studies in first language development* (pp. 339–355). Cambridge: Cambridge University Press.

Chomsky, Noam. (1965). *Aspects of the theory of syntax.* Cambridge, Mass.: MIT Press.

Coleman, Linda. (1983). Semantic and prosodic manipulation in advertising. In Harris, Richard J. (ed.), *Information processing research in advertising* (pp. 217–240). Hillsdale, N.J.: Lawrence Erlbaum.

Comrie, Bernard. (1989). *Language universals and linguistic typology.* Chicago: University of Chicago Press.

Cook, Eung-Do. (1989). Is phonology going haywire in dying languages? Phonological variations in Chipewyan and Sarcee. *Language in Society, 18*: 235–255.

Cook, Guy. (1992). *The discourse of advertising.* London: Routledge.

Cooper, Marilyn M. (1982). Context as vehicle: Implicatures in writing. In Nystrand, Martin (ed.), *What writers know: The language, process, and structure of written discourse* (pp. 105–128). New York: Academic Press.

Corder, S. Pit. (1977). "Simple codes" and the source of the second language learner's initial heuristic hypothesis. *Studies in Second Language Acquisition, 1*: 1–10.

Coulmas, Florian. (1979). On the sociolinguistic relevance of routine formulae. *Journal of Pragmatics, 3*: 239–266.

Coulmas, Florian. (1981). Introduction: Conversational routines. In Coulmas, Florian (ed.), *Conversational routines: Explorations in standardized communication situations and prepatterned speech* (pp. 1–17). The Hague: Mouton.

Cruttenden, Alan. (1977). The acquisition of personal pronouns and language "simplification." *Language and Speech, 20*: 191–197.

Crystal, David, & Davy, Derek. (1969). *Investigating English style.* Bloomington: Indiana University Press.

de Beaugrande, Robert, & Dressler, Wolfgang U. (1981). *Introduction to text linguistics.* London: Longman.

Dixon, Robert M. W. (1971). A method of semantic description. In Steinberg, Danny D., & Jakobowits, Leon A. (eds.), *Semantics: An interdisciplinary reader in philosophy, linguistics, and psychology* (pp. 436–471). Cambridge: Cambridge University Press.

Dorian, Nancy C. (1981). *Language death: The life cycle of a Scottish Gaelic dialect.* Cambridge: Cambridge University Press.

Eisenstein, Miriam, & Starbuck, Robin. (1989). The effect of emotional investment in L2 production. In Gass, Susan M., Madden, Carolyn G., Preston, Dennis R., & Selinker, Larry (eds.), *Variation in second language acquisition: Psycholinguistic issues* (pp. 125–140). Clevedon, England: Multilingual Matters.

Ervin-Tripp, Susan M. (1972). On sociolinguistic rules: Alternation and co-occurrence. In Gumperz, John J., & Hymes, Dell (eds.), *Direction in sociolinguistics* (pp. 213–250). New York: Holt, Rinehart & Winston.

Fathman, Ann. (1977). Similarities and simplification in the interlanguage of second language learners. In Corder, S. Pit, & Roulet, E. (eds.), *The notion of simplification, interlanguages and pidgins and their relation to second language pedagogy* (pp. 30–38). Neuchâtel, Switz.: Faculté des Lettres.

Ferguson, Charles A. (1971). Absence of copula and the notion of simplicity: A study of normal speech, baby talk, foreigner talk and pidgins. In Hymes, Dell (ed.), *Pidginization and creolization of language* (pp. 141–150). Cambridge: Cambridge University Press.

Ferguson, Charles A. (1975). Toward a characterization of English foreigner talk. *Anthropological Linguistics, 17*: 1–14.

Ferguson, Charles A. (1977). Baby talk as a simplified register. In Snow, Catherine E., & Ferguson, Charles A. (eds.), *Talking to children: Language input and acquisition* (pp. 209–233). Cambridge: Cambridge University Press.

Ferguson, Charles A. (1982). Simplified registers and linguistic theory. In Obler, Lorraine K., & Menn, Lise (eds.), *Exceptional language and linguistics* (pp. 49–66). New York: Academic Press.

Ferguson, Charles A. (1983). Sports announcer talk: Syntactic aspects of register variation. *Language in Society, 12*: 153–172.

Ferguson, Charles A. (1985). Special language registers: Editor's introduction. *Discourse Processes, 8*: 391–394.

Ferguson, Charles A. (1994). Dialect, register, and genre: Working assumptions about conventionalization. In Biber, Douglas, & Finegan, Edward (eds.), *Sociolinguistic perspectives on register* (pp. 15–30). New York: Oxford University Press.

Ferguson, Charles A., & DeBose, Charles E. (1977). Simplified registers, broken language, and pidginization. In Valdman, Albert (ed.), *Pidgin and creole linguistics* (pp. 99–125). Bloomington: Indiana University Press.

Finegan, Edward. (1987). On the linguistic forms of prestige: Snobs and slobs using English. In Boardman, Phillip C. (ed.), *The legacy of language* (pp. 146–161). Reno: University of Nevada Press.

Finegan, Edward, & Biber, Douglas. (1986). Two dimensions of linguistic complexity in English. In Connor-Linton, Jeff, Hall, Christopher J., & McGinnis, Mary (eds.), *Social and cognitive perspectives on language* (pp. 1–23). Southern California Occasional Papers in Linguistics, vol. 11. Los Angeles: University of Southern California.

Finegan, Edward, & Biber, Douglas. (1994). Register and social dialect variation: An integrated approach. In Biber, Douglas, & Finegan, Edward (eds.), *Sociolinguistic perspectives on register* (pp. 315–347). New York: Oxford University Press.

Fitzpatrick, Eileen, Bachenko, Joan, & Hindle, Don. (1986). The status of telegraphic sublanguages. In Grishman, Ralph, & Kitteredge, Richard (eds.), *Analyzing language in restricted domains* (pp. 39–51). Hillsdale, N.J.: Lawrence Erlbaum.

Fowler, Roger. (1991). *Language in the news: Discourse and ideology in the press.* London: Routledge.

Fox, Barbara A., & Thompson, Sandra A. (1990). A discourse explanation of the grammar of relative clauses in English conversation. *Language, 66:* 297–316.

Francis, Nelson W. & Kučera, Henry. (1982). *Frequency analysis of English usage: Lexicon and grammar.* Boston: Houghton Mifflin.

Friedrich, Paul. (1988). The unheralded revolution in the sonnet: Toward a generative model. In Tannen, Deborah (ed.), *Linguistics in context: Connecting observation and understanding* (pp. 199–219). Norwood, N.J.: Ablex.

Geis, Michael L. (1982). *The language of television advertising.* New York: Academic Press.

Ghadessy, Mohsen. (1988). The language of written sports commentary: Soccer: A description. In Ghadessy, Mohsen (ed.), *Registers of written English: Situational factors and linguistic features* (pp. 17–51). London: Pinter.

Gibbon, Dafydd. (1985). Context and variation in two-way radio discourse. *Discourse Processes, 8:* 395–419.

Givón, Talmy. (1979). *On understanding grammar.* New York: Academic Press.

Gleitman, Lila R., Newport, Elissa L., & Gleitman, Henry. (1984). The current status of the motherese hypothesis. *Journal of Child Language, 11:* 43–79.

Grice, H. Paul. (1975). Logic and conversation. In Cole, Peter, & Morgan, Jerry L. (eds.), *Syntax and semantics, vol. 3: Speech acts* (pp. 41–58). New York: Academic Press.

Gunter, Richard. (1963). Elliptical sentences in American English. *Lingua, 12:* 137–150.

Hakuta, Kenji. (1974). Prefabricated patterns and the emergence of structure in second language acquisition. *Language Learning, 24:* 287–298.

Halliday, M. A. K. (1967). *Grammar, society and the noun.* London: H. K. Lewis for University College.

Halliday, M. A. K. (1985). *An introduction to functional grammar.* London: Edward Arnold.

Halliday, M. A. K. (1989). *Spoken and written language.* Oxford: Oxford University Press.

Halliday, M. A. K. (1991). Corpus studies and probabilistic grammar. In Aijmer, Karin, & Altenberg, Bengt (eds.), *English corpus linguistics* (pp. 30–43). London: Longman.

Halliday, M. A. K., & Hasan, Ruqaiya. (1976). *Cohesion in English.* London: Longman.

Halliday, M. A. K., & Hasan, Ruqaiya. (1989). *Language, context, and text: Aspects of language in a social-semiotic perspective.* Oxford: Oxford University Press.

Hatch, Evelyn M. (1983a). *Psycholinguistics: A second language perspective.* Cambridge, Mass: Newbury House.

Hatch, Evelyn M. (1983b). Simplified input and second language acquisition. In Andersen, Roger W. (ed.), *Pidginization and creolization as language acquisition* (pp. 64–86). Rowley, Mass.: Newbury House.

Hatch, Evelyn M., & Lazaraton, Ann. (1991). *The research manual: Design and statistics for applied linguistics.* New York: Newbury House.

Haviland, John B. (1979). Guugu Yimidhirr brother-in-law language. *Language in Society,* 3: 365–393.

Hawkins, John A. (1978). *Definiteness and indefiniteness: A study in reference and grammaticality prediction.* London: Croom Helm.

Hawkins, John A. (1990). On (in)definite articles: Implicatures and (un)grammaticality prediction. Unpublished manuscript, University of Southern California, Los Angeles.

He, Agnes W. (1992). Constituting knowledge systems and power relations through modality: Cases from academic counseling encounters. Paper presented at the Fourteenth Annual Meeting of AAAL, Seattle, February 28–March 2.

Heine, Bernd, Claudi, Ulrike & Hünnemeyer, Friederike. (1991). *Grammaticalization: A conceptual framework.* Chicago: University of Chicago Press.

Hoey, Michael. (1983). *On the surface of discourse.* London: Allen & Unwin.

Holm, John A. (1988). *Pidgins and creoles* (vols. 1 & 2). Cambridge: Cambridge University Press.

Hopper, Paul J. (1988). Emergent grammar and the a priori grammar postulate. In Tannen, Deborah (ed.), *Linguistics in context: Connecting observation and understanding* (pp. 117–134). Norwood, N.J.: Ablex.

Huddleston, Rodney. (1984). *Introduction to the grammar of English.* Cambridge: Cambridge University Press.

Hudson, Richard A. (1980). *Sociolinguistics.* Cambridge: Cambridge University Press.

Janda, Richard D. (1985). Note-taking as a simplified register. *Discourse Processes,* 8: 437–454.

Janicki, Karol. (1990). *Toward non-essentialist sociolinguistics.* Berlin: Mouton.

Johansson, Stig, & Hofland, Knut. (1989). *Frequency analysis of English vocabulary and grammar* (vols. 1 & 2). Oxford: Clarendon Press.

Johnstone, Barbara. (1987). An introduction. *Text,* 7: 205–214.

Kaye, Jonathan. (1989). *Phonology: A cognitive view.* Hillsdale, N.J.: Lawrence Erlbaum.

Kemper, Susan, Jackson, James D., Cheung, Hintat, & Anagnopoulos,

Cheryl A. (1993). Enhancing older adults' reading comprehension. *Discourse Processes, 16*: 405–428.

Kjellmer, Göran. (1990). Patterns of collocability. In Aarts, Jan, & Meijs, Willem (eds.), *Theory and practice in corpus linguistics* (pp. 163–178). Amsterdam: Rodopi.

Kjellmer, Göran. (1991). A mint of phrases. In Aijmer, Karin, & Altenberg, Bengt (eds.), *English corpus linguistics: Studies in honour of Jan Svartvik* (pp. 111–127). London: Longman.

Klein, Wolfgang. (1986). *Second language acquisition*. Cambridge: Cambridge University Press.

Krashen, Stephen D., & Scarcella, Robin. (1978). On routines and patterns in language acquisition and performance. *Language Learning, 28*: 283–300.

Labov, William. (1969). Contraction, deletion, and inherent variability of the English copula. *Language, 45*: 715–762.

Labov, William. (1972). *Sociolinguistics patterns*. Philadelphia: University of Pennsylvania Press.

Lakoff, Robin T. (1982). Persuasive discourse and ordinary conversation, with examples from advertising. In Tannen, Deborah (ed.), *Analyzing discourse: Text and talk* (pp. 25–42). Georgetown University Round Table on Languages and Linguistics. Washington, D.C.: Georgetown University Press.

Larsen-Freeman, Diane & Long, Michael H. 1991. *An introduction to second language research*. London: Longman.

Lautamatti, Liisa. (1987). Observations on the development of the topic of simplified discourse. In Connor, Ulla M., & Kaplan, Robert B. (eds.), *Writing across languages: Analysis of L2 text* (pp. 87–114). Reading, Mass.: Addison-Wesley.

Lavandera, Beatriz R. (1978). Where does the sociolinguistic variable stop? *Language in Society, 7*: 171–182.

Leech, Geoffrey N. (1966). *English in advertising*. London: Longman.

Leow, Ronald P. (1993). To simplify or not to simplify: A look at intake. *Studies in Second Language Acquisition, 15*: 333–355.

Levelt, Willem. J. M. (1989). *Speaking: From intention to articulation*. Cambridge, Mass.: MIT Press.

Levinson, Steven C. (1989). Review of Sperber and Wilson's "Relevance." *Journal of Linguistics 25*: 455–472.

Mårdh, Ingrid. (1980). *Headlinese: On the grammar of English front page headlines*. Malmö, Sweden: CWK Gleerup.

Matthews, P. H. (1981). *Syntax*. Cambridge: Cambridge University Press.

Meisel, Jürgen M. (1977). Linguistic simplification: A study of immigrant workers' speech and foreigner talk. In Corder, S. Pit, & Roulet, E. (eds.), *The notion of simplification, interlanguages and pidgins and their relation to second language pedagogy* (pp. 88–113). Neuchâtel, Switz.: Faculté des Lettres.

Meisel, Jürgen M. (1983a). A linguistic encounter of the third kind, or, will the non-real interfere with what the non-learner does? Reply to discussants. In Andersen, Roger W. (ed.), *Pidginization and creolization as language acquisition* (pp. 196–209). Rowley, Mass.: Newbury House.

Meisel, Jürgen M. (1983b). Strategies of second language acquisition: More than one kind of simplification. In Andersen, Roger W. (ed.), *Pidginization and creolization as language acquisition* (pp. 120–157). Rowley, Mass.: Newbury House.

Miecznikowski, Anna, & Andersen, Elaine S. (1986). From formulaic to analyzed speech: Two systems or one? In Connor-Linton, Jeff, Hall, Christopher J., & McGinnis, Mary (eds.), *Social and cognitive perspectives on language* (pp. 181–202). Southern California Occasional Papers in Linguistics, vol. 11. Los Angeles: University of Southern California.

Milroy, James, & Milroy, Lesley. (1985). *Authority in language: Investigating language prescription and standardisation.* London: Routledge & Kegan Paul.

Milroy, Lesley. (1987). *Observing and analysing natural language.* Oxford: Blackwell.

Mühlhaüsler, Peter. (1974). *Pidginization and simplification of language.* Canberra, Austr.: Pacific Linguistics, B26.

Mühlhaüsler, Peter. (1986). *Pidgin and creole linguistics.* Oxford: Blackwell.

Mühlhaüsler, Peter, & Harré, Rom. (1990). *Pronouns and people: The linguistic construction of social and personal identity.* Oxford: Blackwell.

Nair, Rukmini B. (1992). Gender, genre, and generative grammar: Deconstructing the matrimonial column. In Toolan, Michael J. (ed.), *Language, text and context* (pp. 227–254). London: Routledge.

Nash, Walter. (1985). *The language of humor.* London: Longman.

Norrick, Neal R. (1987). Functions of repetition in conversation. *Text,* 7: 245–264.

Ochs, Elinor. (1979). Planned and unplanned discourse. In Givón, Talmy (ed.), *Syntax and semantics, vol. 12: Discourse and syntax* (pp. 51–58). New York: Academic Press.

Ochs, Elinor, & Schieffelin, Bambi B. (1984). Language acquisition and socialization: Three developmental stories and their implications. In Shweder, Richard A., & LeVine, Robert A. (eds.), *Culture and its acquisition* (pp. 276–320). New York: Cambridge University Press.

Ochs, Elinor, & Schieffelin, Bambi B. (1989). Language has a heart. *Text,* 9: 7–25.

O'Donnell, William R., & Todd, Loreto. (1991). *Variety in contemporary English.* London: Harper/Collins Academic.

Pawley, Andrew. (1986). Lexicalization. In Tannen, Deborah (ed.), *Lan-

guage and linguistics: The interdependence of theory, data, and application (pp. 98–120). Georgetown University Round Table on Languages and Linguistics. Washington, D.C.: Georgetown University Press.

Pawley, Andrew, & Syder, Frances H. (1983a). Natural selection in syntax: Notes on adaptive variation and change in vernacular and literary grammar. *Journal of Pragmatics, 7*: 551–579.

Pawley, Andrew, & Syder, Frances H. (1983b). Two puzzles for linguistic theory: Nativelike selection and nativelike fluency. In Richards, Jack C., & Schmidt, Richard W. (eds.), *Language and communication* (pp. 191–225). London: Longman.

Peters, Ann M. (1983). *The units of language acquisition*. Cambridge: Cambridge University Press.

Philips, Susan U. (1985). Strategies of clarification in judges' use of language: From the written to the spoken. *Discourse Processes, 8*: 421–436.

Renouf, Antoinette, & Sinclair, John McH. (1991). Collocational frameworks in English. In Aijmer, Karin, & Altenberg, Bengt (eds.), *English corpus linguistics* (pp. 128–143). London: Longman.

Roberts, Richard M., & Kreuz, Roger J. (1993). Nonstandard discourse and its coherence. *Discourse Processes, 16*: 451–464.

Robertson, Fiona A. (1987). *Airspeak: Radiotelephony communication for pilots*. New York: Prentice Hall.

Romaine, Suzanne. (1988). *Pidgin and creole languages*. London: Longman.

Romaine, Suzanne. (1994). On the creation and expansion of registers: Sports reporting in Tok Pisin. In Biber, Douglas, & Finegan, Edward (eds.), *Sociolinguistic perspectives on register* (pp. 59–81). New York: Oxford University Press.

Samarin, William J. (1971). Salient and substantive pidginization. In Hymes, Dell (ed.), *Pidginization and creolization of languages* (pp. 117–140). Cambridge: Cambridge University Press.

Schiffrin, Deborah. (1987). *Discourse markers*. Cambridge: Cambridge University Press.

Schleppegrell, Mary J. (1992). Subordination and linguistic complexity. *Discourse Processes, 15*: 117–131.

Schmidt, Annette. (1985). *Young people's Dyirbal: An example of language death from Australia*. Cambridge: Cambridge University Press.

Schumann, John H. (1978). *The pidginization process: A model for second language acquisition*. Rowley, Mass.: Newbury House.

Shatz, Marilyn, & Gelman, Rochel. (1977). Beyond syntax: The influence of conversational constraints on speech modification. In Snow, Catherine E., & Ferguson, Charles A. (eds.), *Talking to children: Language input and acquisition* (pp. 189–198). Cambridge: Cambridge University Press.

Shuy, Roger W., & Larkin, Donald L. (1978). Linguistic considerations in the simplification/clarification of insurance policy language. *Discourse Processes, 1*: 305–321.

Sinclair, John McH. (1987). Collocation: A progress report. In Steele, Ross, & Threadgold, Terry (eds.), *Language topics: Essays in honour of Michael Halliday* (vol. 1, pp. 319–331). Amsterdam: John Benjamins.

Sinclair, John McH. (1988). Compressed English. In Ghadessy, Mohsen (ed.), *Registers of written English: Situational factors and linguistic features* (pp. 130–136). London: Pinter.

Snow, Catherine E. (1986). Conversations with children. In Fletcher, Paul, & Garman, Michael (eds.), *Language acquisition: Studies in first language development* (pp. 69–89). Cambridge: Cambridge University Press.

Sperber, Dan, & Wilson, Deirdre. (1986). *Relevance: Communication and cognition.* Oxford: Blackwell.

Straumann, H. (1935). *Newspaper headlines: A study in linguistic method.* London: Allen & Unwin.

Swales, John M. (1990). *Genre analysis: English in academic and research settings.* Cambridge: Cambridge University Press.

Tanaka, Keiko. (1994). *Advertising language: A pragmatic approach to advertisements in Britain and Japan.* London: Routledge.

Tannen, Deborah. (1982a). Oral and literate strategies in spoken and written narratives. *Language, 58*: 1–21.

Tannen, Deborah. (1982b). The oral/literate continuum in discourse. In Tannen, Deborah (ed.), *Spoken and written language: Exploring orality and literacy* (pp. 1–16). Norwood, N.J.: Ablex.

Tannen, Deborah. (1985). Relative focus on involvement in oral and written discourse. In Olson, David R., Torrance, Nancy, & Hildyard, Angela (eds.), *Literacy, language and learning: The nature and consequences of reading and writing* (pp. 123–147). Cambridge: Cambridge University Press.

Tannen, Deborah. (1987). Repetition in conversation as spontaneous formulaicity. *Text, 7*: 215–243.

Tannen, Deborah. (1989). *Talking voices: Repetition, dialogue, and imagery in conversational discourse.* Cambridge: Cambridge University Press.

Todd, Loreto. (1990). *Pidgins and creoles.* London: Routledge & Kegan Paul.

Toolan, Michael J. (1988). The language of press advertising. In Ghadessy, Mohsen (ed.), *Registers of written English: Situational factors and linguistic features* (pp. 52–64). London: Pinter.

Uspensky, B. A., & Zhivov, V. M. (1977). Center-periphery opposition and language universals. *Linguistics, 196*: 5–24.

van Dijk, Teun A. (1988). *News as discourse.* Hillsdale, N.J.: Lawrence Erlbaum.

Verschueren, Jef. (1981). The semantics of forgotten routines. In Coulmas, Florian (ed.), *Conversational routine: Explorations in standardized communication situations and prepatterned speech* (pp. 133–153). The Hague: Mouton.

Vestergaard, Torben, & Schrøder, Kim. (1985). *The language of advertising*. Oxford: Blackwell.

Williamson, Judith. (1983). *Decoding advertisements: Ideology and meaning in advertising*. London: Marion Boyars.

INDEX

abbreviations, 21–3, 33, 36, 81–2, 93–7, 157, 180-3, 189n. *See also* contractions
adjectives
  attributive, 8, 98, 100, 126, 152, 155
  predicative, 8, 152
  See also collocation
ads, matrimonial, 30, 35–6, 127, 189n
advertising
  classified, linguistic nature of, 8, 16, 20, 23–5, 30–1
  discourse of, 21, 23–4, 26–30, 37
  display, 26, 29, 31, 40, 121
  television, 26, 28, 37, 93, 187n
affect, 9, 15, 53–5, 57, 66, 113, 164–5
alliteration, 36, 74, 103
ambiguity, 24, 29, 83–4, 88, 149–50
articles
  definite, 41, 43–5, 109–10, 134, 140, 144–6
  indefinite, 45–9, 111–2, 134, 137, 146–7, 149
auxiliaries, 16–8, 26, 39–40, 52–4, 57–9. *See also* modals

baby talk, 12–3, 18–9, 40, 59, 71, 163–5, 174, 187n

capitalization, 50
chaining, lexical, 31, 66, 69, 72, 75–6, 78–81, 150. *See also* parataxis

clusters of linguistic features, 5–8, 20, 25, 148, 151, 153, 155
coherence, 28, 72, 81, 88
cohesion, 15, 92–3, 190n
collocation
  as framework, 108, 120, 131, 189n
  definition of, 97–9
  with adjectives, 103–5
  with nouns, 100–3
  with particles, 54, 99, 107–8
  with verbs, 105–7
communication apprehension, 30
competence
  communicative, 170, 172
  grammatical, 7, 37, 91, 99, 168–71
  See also innateness
complexity, syntactic, 3, 5–6, 10, 14, 77, 143, 150, 156, 168
compounding, lexical, 31, 58, 70–1, 89
comprehension of simplified texts, 3–6, 9, 23–9, 77, 81, 144, 146. *See also* processing of information
compression of linguistic form, 15–6, 21, 44, 81, 110. *See also* constraints
constituents, syntactic, 82, 85–6, 189n
constraints on classified ad writers
  cognitive, 13, 16, 79, 90, 92, 99, 168
  editorial, 24, 38, 70, 90, 95–6, 120–3, 130–1, 184, 189n

204

spatial, 9, 15–6, 20–3, 32, 40, 43–5, 54, 56–7, 66–7, 69–75, 77–9, 81, 90, 94–5, 97–8, 107–8, 140, 142, 146, 169–71, 191n
temporal, 9, 15, 24, 90
See also function, production
content, propositional, 6, 15, 94, 120, 148
context
  dependence on, 4–7, 28–9, 82–4, 144–5, 160, 171
  obligatory, 11, 16–7, 39, 41, 88, 130–2, 170
  shared, 43, 52, 81, 98, 145–6, 155
  textual, 16–7, 44–5, 59–60, 66, 88, 147, 149, 153, 167
contractions, 34, 188n. See also abbreviations
conventionalization
  as linguistic form, 6, 34, 36–7, 43–4, 52, 144
  as process, 13, 16–8, 20–2, 82, 90–3, 120–1, 160, 168–70, 172, 174, 187–9n
  See also norms
conversation, functional correlates of, 8, 66, 91, 120, 149, 151
cooperation between writer and reader, 28–9, 44, 61, 82, 145, 150, 165
coordination
  additive, 72–6
  clausal, 75–6
  contrastive, 76–7
  in collocations, 118–20
  lexical, 72–5
  role in simplified texts, 3, 13, 40
copulas, 10, 12, 16, 31, 40, 58–63, 87–8, 116–7, 134, 138–9, 152–4
corpus
  Brown, 40–1, 45, 49, 53–4, 57, 59, 64, 67, 72, 77, 132, 137–40, 188n

London-Oslo-Bergen (LOB), 40–1, 45, 49, 53–4, 57, 59, 64, 67, 72, 77, 99–100, 102–4, 107–8, 132, 137–40, 188–90n
selection of, 31–7, 178
See also linguistics
creativity, lexical, 26–7, 48, 61, 70–1, 74, 88–91, 104, 114–5, 119, 169–71

deixis. See reference
deletion of redundant material, 9, 11, 22, 43, 51, 87, 89, 113, 156, 165, 167, 190n
determiners, 115–6
diaries, 16, 190n
discourse
  analysis, 7, 90, 120
  structure, 7, 25, 29–31, 103, 105–6, 120–32, 174, 189–90n
disjunction, 24, 26, 89
distancing, social, 18, 143, 161, 163–4
documents, official, 151, 154

elaboration, syntactic, 4, 9–12, 14, 16–7, 21–4, 35, 39–41, 81, 87–8, 96–7, 119, 130–4, 140–3, 157, 167–72, 174–5, 189n. See also reduction

feedback, 8, 12–3, 17, 24, 161, 163–4
fiction, 26
foreigner talk, 13, 18–9, 40, 59, 62, 91, 163–5, 174, 187n
form, underlying, 5, 31, 51, 87, 89, 113, 156, 165, 167, 189n
fragmentation, textual, 56–7, 69, 77, 86, 152. See also integration

function
　as determinant of linguistic form, 5–10, 13–4, 16–7, 21–7, 35, 52, 81, 90, 99, 108, 130–3, 143–4, 154, 156, 161–74 (*See also* constraints, production)
　as dimension of interaction, 143–59, 162–6
　　implicitness v. explicitness, 147, 149, 151–3, 155–60, 169, 174
　　involvement v. information, 146–9, 151–3, 157–60, 164, 169, 174, 190n
　communicative, 4–6, 15, 52, 57, 66, 81, 90, 92, 142–4, 151, 155, 165, 168

genre, 7–8, 26, 28, 30, 148. *See also* language; register; style; text type; writing
grammar
　generative, 7, 9, 91, 169, 171, 173, 187n
　literary, 10–1, 14, 16–8, 31, 39–40, 43, 45–6, 49–51, 68–70, 78–9, 86–9, 149–50, 168, 170–2
　probabilistic, 7, 99, 173
　vernacular, 66, 149–50
grammaticality, 9, 59, 105, 167, 172–3, 188n

headlines, 15–6, 18, 24–6, 49, 164–5, 173
hyphenation, 33, 70

idea units, 154
ideology, 29–31, 127–9, 131, 174, 189n
idiomaticity, 43–4, 65, 78, 93–4, 97–8, 111–2
inflection, 10, 54, 61, 85

innateness, 19–20, 22, 90, 140, 143, 163, 166–70. *See also* competence
integration, textual, 14, 66, 69, 80, 105–8, 126, 143, 150–2, 154. *See also* fragmentation
intensifiers, 104, 130
interaction between writer and reader, 4, 6, 8, 24, 49–50, 53, 149, 163

judges' clarifications, 14, 163

language
　acquisition of, 14, 18–9, 49, 57, 170
　block, 24
　death of, 14
　planned, 6, 8, 17–8, 23–4, 67, 89, 120, 150, 152, 163–5
　spoken, characteristics of, 3, 8, 26, 52–3, 72, 89, 163, 166, 187n
　written, characteristics of, 6, 8–10, 20, 22–3, 52, 70, 72, 78–9, 89, 91, 107, 120, 150, 152, 154–5, 163, 172, 187n
　See also genre; register; style; text type; writing
length of classified ads, 32–4, 134, 137–9, 158, 190n
letters
　business, 8, 120, 151
　personal, 8, 153
lexicalization, 58, 71, 74, 112, 117–8
limericks, 17, 165
linguistics
　computational, 7, 20, 25, 99, 173 (*See also* corpus)
　critical, 30

markedness theory, 10–1
methodologies
  qualitative, 93
  quantitative, 27, 39, 72, 93, 96, 144, 188n
modals, 31, 54–7, 113–5, 130–1, 134, 153–4, 188n. See also auxiliaries

negation
  analytic, 57–8
  role in simplified texts, 31, 40, 52–3, 57–9, 115–6, 131, 188n
  synthetic, 53, 57–8
nominalization, 3, 8, 14, 26, 80, 113, 154
norms, 32, 92, 120, 131, 189n. See also conventionalization
note-taking, 16–7, 24, 37, 152, 163–5

parallelism, 108, 119, 152
parataxis, 10, 72, 84, 132. See also chaining
passivization, 56, 60, 106, 120, 122, 128, 154
phonology, 19, 28, 119, 133, 172
pidgins, 5, 10–4, 18–9, 40, 57, 59, 62, 71, 163–4
Plain English, 4
pragmatics, 5, 27–31, 49, 103, 167, 169
prepatterning, 65, 89, 91–3, 98, 108–9, 111–2, 114–5, 131–2, 154, 156, 168–70, 174
prepositions, 31, 40–1, 62–6, 97, 106–7, 117–8, 134, 139–40, 152–6
processing of information, 5–8, 28–9, 111, 127, 154, 165–8. See also comprehension

production of classified ads
  capacity for, 3, 10, 19–20
  simplified, 3, 5–6, 9, 11, 23–4, 71, 84, 90, 92, 142–3, 147, 156, 163, 167–72
  See also constraints; function; register; simplification
pronouns
  demonstrative, 148
  personal, 16, 49–53, 88, 112–3, 134, 137, 148–9, 153, 190n
  possessive, 43, 47, 49, 51–2, 83
psycholinguistics, 5, 16, 28, 154, 166
punctuation, 25, 34, 50, 73, 178, 180

reduction, syntactic, 15–7, 22, 39, 43, 70, 89, 160, 167. See also elaboration
redundancy, 4, 76, 84, 94, 118, 169
reference
  assignment of, 29, 43–4, 49–50, 52, 61–2, 109, 112, 145–6, 150–1, 155
  dependence on, 25, 44, 50–1, 61, 82, 148, 157–8
  endophoric, 41, 144
  exophoric, 41, 88, 144
  underspecification of, 82–3, 88, 145, 150
  unique, 43–5, 146, 190n
register
  avoidance, 18, 164
  economy, 15–7, 57, 62, 81, 84, 160–1, 163–8
  features of, 5–8, 37, 132–4, 143–4, 172
  handicap, 11–5, 70, 160–1, 163–5, 167–8
  markers of, 37, 56, 81, 89, 92, 95, 119, 131, 133, 154, 174
  mother-in-law, 18
  simplified, 5–11, 23, 91, 160–6, 177

register (*continued*)
  variation, 5–8, 20, 22–3, 26–7, 132–3, 154, 171–3 (*See also* variation)
  See also genre; language; style; text type; writing
relativization
  hierarchy of, 67
  role in simplified texts, 14, 40–1, 50–1, 64, 66–9, 80, 85, 113, 138, 149–51
relevance theory, 28–9
repetition, 27, 74, 90–2, 97, 99–100, 111, 119–20, 130–1, 147, 154, 169
restriction, semantic, 10, 13, 155

sequencing
  alphabetical, 105–6, 118
  of information (*See* discourse structure)
simplicity. *See* simplification
simplification
  characterizations of, 3–5, 8–11, 160–1, 177
  elaborative, 11
  restrictive, 11
  See also production; register; simplified
situation as determinant of linguistic form. *See* function
sociolinguistics, 21, 90, 92, 133, 161, 166
socialization, 92, 130
sonnets, 17
speeches, formal, 149
sports announcer talk, 17, 37, 152, 163
stance, 9, 15, 27, 54, 66, 113, 122
standardization, 38, 82, 92, 116, 184
style, 15, 17, 27–9, 47, 53, 140, 164, 169, 187n. *See also* genre; language; register; text type; writing

subordination, 3, 10, 14–5, 40, 73, 77–9, 88–9

telephone messages, 16, 173, 190n
text type, 8, 25–6, 90, 96, 140, 142, 155, 163. *See also* genre; language; register; style; writing
thematization, 122
type-to-token ratios, 96, 97, 155, 157–8, 189n
typography, 33, 74, 188n

variables, sociolinguistic, 133
variation
  diachronic, 170, 173
  panchronic, 170
  paradigmatic, 11, 63
  synchronic, 20, 170, 173
  See also register
verbs
  finite, 75
  private, 79, 107
  See also collocation

word
  classes, 97, 99, 101, 119
  counts, 33–4, 38, 40–1, 188–9n
  order, 10, 13
  types
    content, 63, 95–8, 133, 142, 191n
    function, 11, 16, 21, 23, 26, 40, 52, 63, 93–4, 108, 110, 119, 132–4, 139–40, 144, 157–8, 166, 174
writing
  academic, 120, 122, 149, 155
  didactic, 14–5
  journalistic, 25, 30, 121–2, 154–5
  scientific, 26
  See also genre; language; register; style; text type